D1454332

LIVING CATHOLICISM

LIVING CATHOLICISM

RODERICK STRANGE

DARTON · LONGMAN + TODD

First published in 2001 by
Darton, Longman and Todd Ltd
1 Spencer Court
140-142 Wandsworth High Street
London SW18 4JJ

ISBN 0–232–52291–X

A catalogue record for this book is available from the
British Library.

Designed by Sandie Boccacci
Phototypeset in 11^1/$_4$/14pt Bembo by
Intype London Limited
Printed and bound in Great Britain by
Page Bros, Norwich, Norfolk

For
Anne Barker.

Contents

Acknowledgements

SCRIPTURAL references have been taken generally from the Revised Standard Version, copyright © Division of Christian Education of the Churches of Christ in the United States of America, 1946, 1952, 1971, but sometimes from the New Revised Standard Version, Anglicized Edition, copyright © Division of Christian Education of the Churches of Christ in the United States of America, 1989, 1995.

Quotations from the documents of the Second Vatican Council come from the edition by Austin Flannery OP (Dublin, 1975).

Preface

(i)

ACCORDING to tradition, St John was the only apostle who was not martyred. In old age he lived in exile on the island of Patmos. Worn down by years, his teaching was reduced to a single phrase: 'Little children, love one another. Little children, love one another', which he is supposed to have repeated over and over again. I was reminded of this story some years ago. I had officiated at a wedding and afterwards, at the reception, the bride's father referred to it, but he added a further, vital element. St John's words, he remarked, did not demonstrate mental failure. He had not become senile. In this simple phrase, drawing on his experience at the end of a long life, he had summed up the pure essence of the gospel. At its core is a command to love.

One day, during my time as university chaplain at Oxford, an undergraduate who had not managed to come to mass that day, asked another what I had been preaching about. 'What he always preaches about,' came the laughing reply, 'when he isn't preaching about love.' It became a focus for banter, the idea that I only had two sermons; but the underlying point was serious and I took it as a compliment: it was the constant emphasis on love. It must be so. Loving lies at the heart of living Catholicism. It lies at the heart of this book.

An earlier book, *The Catholic Faith*, was more doctrinal.[1] It was written principally for Catholic undergraduates. I had found that many who came to the chaplaincy had a strong faith and were committed to prayer, but, when questioned about their beliefs, found themselves at a loss. Drawing on material I had used in homilies and various talks I had been invited to give, I tried to put together an account of Catholicism which could help them. At the same time, I hoped that what I offered might be useful to those who were not Catholics, but had an interest in Catholicism, for those of my own generation, the parents of undergraduates, who had not quite managed to come to terms with the Second Vatican Council, and for those Catholics who were older still, and who had never been properly prepared for change at all. A further reason for writing was to try to give shape and coherence to material which I had been using a great deal. As I did so, I found three basic principles emerging even more clearly than I had expected.

The first concerned the Father. It stated that the Father sent his Son to reconcile the world to himself. This mystery of the Father's love is celebrated at Christmas and reconciliation is to be discovered in the relationship revealed between the divine and the human in the birth of Jesus: the two natures are perfectly respected and perfectly united. It is the principle of the in-carnation. The second principle brings before us the way that reconciliation was accomplished: it was made known by a revel-ation of unreserved, unconditional love. The entire existence of Jesus of Nazareth proclaims that love, but it was shown supremely by his acceptance of death on the cross and his being raised from the dead. This mystery of love is celebrated in Holy Week and at Easter. It is the principle of death and resurrection, of the paschal mystery. And the third principle is based on the re-alization that identity and self-knowledge are inseparable; in other words, in order for an individual or a community to be secure in their identity, they have to have at least sufficient knowledge of who they are. This identity was granted to those gathered in the upper room fifty days after Jesus had been raised, when, through the presence of the Holy Spirit, they came to know themselves as the body of Christ, as the Church. We celebrate the birth of the Church at Pentecost. These three principles follow from our faith in God who is Father and Son and Spirit and are celebrated each year in our liturgy, at Christmas, Easter, and Pentecost.

This fundamental structure allowed me to present an account of our understanding about Jesus and the Church, the sacraments

and virtues, our teaching on Mary and our belief in God as
One and Three. The approach was doctrinal, but it opened
doors to spirituality. The key is to be found in the faithful love
of Jesus, his love for his Father and his love for us. The Father's
love seeks the reconciliation we need because of sin; by sin we
have separated ourselves from God. Jesus so loves the Father that
he came to accomplish that reconciliation, out of love for his
Father and for us. That book ended in a call to prayer. And this
one begins from that point. I have called it *Living Catholicism*.
The title is not meant to suggest Catholicism and current affairs,
but something broader and deeper, a Catholicism come alive
and how we are to live it. It has to be living in both senses. It
has taken a long time to write.

Shortly before I left Oxford in 1989, I was invited to preach
a retreat to a group gathered in Lourdes. The retreat was to
last a week and I was asked to give two talks each day, fourteen
in all. It was a considerable challenge and it forced me to organize
the ideas I had been putting together since preparing *The Catholic
Faith*. It was a very satisfying exercise. The origins of this book
can be traced to that retreat.

In the retreat I spoke from notes, but I planned to write up
the text during my sabbatical later that year. It was not to be. I
wrote four chapters in draft and then found that I had different
calls upon my time. Given other responsibilities, I have managed
only now to return to it. But I believe the delay has been
beneficial. The 1990s has been a period of rich reflection, particularly with regard to the Church; for example, only now has
the understanding of the Church as communion emerged more
clearly, while during that time I have been a parish priest, the
director of the Religious Education Service for the Diocese of
Shrewsbury, chairman of the National Conference of Priests,
and now a seminary rector. And while the earlier book was
more doctrinal, but led to spirituality, here the emphasis is on
spirituality, but a spirituality built on a firm doctrinal foundation.
Where the earlier book began with teaching and moved on to
recognize its interior aspect, here we explore the inner life so as

to discover its implications for discipleship. Let me sketch the path we will follow.

(ii)

We begin with the need for watchfulness. We have to be perceptive, alert to God's presence. That watchfulness and the longing which inspires it, lead us into prayer, and our understanding of prayer itself becomes more profound when we contemplate Jesus at prayer. It shows us something of his inner life, the intimacy of his relationship with the Father. That love is revealed specifically in his readiness to accept the consequences of this loving, whatever they may be; and so we are brought to reflect, so to speak, from within on the passion and death of Jesus. And following the same line, we contemplate his resurrection. In all this, we try to realize what it means for us to share in this loving and suffering and rising. We are led to consider what it means to be the people of God, the body of Christ, members of the Church.

God meets us in love in the experiences of our ordinary lives. That truth is vital. It follows from our conviction about the Word made flesh: when the Son became human, he became an ordinary human being; his humanity was exactly like ours. Nevertheless, we discover in providence and miracle privileged moments in which God's love is revealed to us. We pause to consider them and to realize the way they are a part of the larger pattern.

From these matters, we move on to consider the invitation we have received to share in God's life, to be holy as the Lord our God is holy, and so to be his disciples. We reflect upon the sacraments of eucharist and reconciliation to appreciate more vividly the way we are offered support to sustain us as followers of Jesus, and then we examine what it means to put love into practice and be living witnesses of the gospel. The love that emerged as the key to understanding doctrine more deeply comes to be recognized as the indispensable core of living Catholicism.

The range this book covers is considerable. To state the whole matter briefly, from contemplating Jesus, we try to understand more clearly our vocation to holiness and discipleship, so that we may make the love which is at the very centre of this whole way of living, real and active. There are further books which could be written on each chapter and many other themes and aspects could have been included. No one book on living Catholicism could ever be exhaustive. My hope is that this book will give people who like reading, but would not perhaps have the time to read a series of books, an accessible introduction to what it means so to believe in Catholicism that it becomes truly alive day by day. In this way they may come to recognize what it means to pray, to gaze on Jesus and learn from him, to share his life, as an individual and as a member of his body, the Church, and so to live with unreserved love. Once again, I have written for Catholics and non-Catholics alike, but with Catholics principally in mind, so that those who are not Catholics need not fear that what is presented here has been in some way doctored specially for them. Our generation has a thirst for spiritual things which will not be quenched by the sweetly superficial. There is a longing to drink deep. It may be that, by beginning here, they will be encouraged to go further. That is my hope.

(iii)

The book draws upon my own experience of what it means to believe and try to live this life, but it is not autobiographical. I have been personal only to illustrate the demands of discipleship, not to define them. One individual's experience could never exhaust the possibilities offered by these mysteries. To live Catholic faith and life can never be a matter of private enterprise. We are influenced at every turn by the people who have guided and helped us, by those whom we have tried to serve and those

who have taken care of us. There are many to whom I owe
debts of gratitude.

I must thank, first of all, Barbara Davies who invited me to
Lourdes to preach that retreat in March 1989 and so supplied
the reason for attempting to bring this material together. Nine
years later, when I had rather ground to a halt, Bishop Brian
Noble of Shrewsbury, my own bishop, encouraged me to begin
again and has offered constant support to my efforts. Both in
their different ways have instigated this work. Others have provided me with notable examples of living Catholicism: the
chaplaincy community in Oxford, the parishioners of St Paul's
in Hyde where I was able to enjoy six memorably happy years,
and then those at English Martyrs' in Wallasey where I had also
been an assistant priest from 1974 to 1977. I was only allowed
two brief years with them before being invited to come here to
the Beda College in Rome: working with men from more than
twenty countries across the English-speaking world, who in later
life seek to serve the Church as ordained priests, has also been
a blessing for me. I pay tribute very gladly as well to Sr Catherine
Darby SND, Paddy Rylands, Rita Price, Nicholas Kern, and Fr
David Roberts, my colleagues in the Religious Education
Service of the Shrewsbury Diocese and also to many others
engaged in the same work in the different dioceses of England
and Wales; I have learnt a great deal from them. And it was a
privilege to be a member of the National Conference of Priests
for eight years and in particular to be elected to serve as its
Chairman from 1994 to 1997. I wish to acknowledge my debt.

When I began to prepare the book for publication seriously
and contacted Darton, Longman and Todd, Morag Reeve
encouraged me at once and, when Brendan Walsh succeeded her,
he maintained the encouragement and showed great patience as
a deadline slipped by. He offered me steady, practical advice so
that I could bring the work to completion. And while writing,
Fr Paul Murray OP kept me enthused, Fr Andrew Faley gave me
his comments on the chapters one by one, as they were drafted,
and Fr Mark Coleridge read the work as a whole at the end.

Assistance of that kind is always invaluable, but particularly when, as here, the writing has to be secondary to other responsibilities. I am grateful to them all and accept the blame for any remaining blunders.

All these people have been involved directly in the production of this book, some more closely than others, but they have all contributed. Besides them, however, there has been a host of people, my mother and my sisters, Jill and Alison, the Ashby family at large and Philippe Taupin in particular at whose home in Umbria I corrected the final typescript, and many other friends whose kindness, generosity, and love have never failed me. They have supplied the rich soil from which a work like this can grow. There are too many to name, but I hold them in love and thank them all. And I reserve a word of particular thanks for Brian and Anne Barker and their daughters, Camilla, Ned, and Felicity, who for many years have so often welcomed me into their home. This book is dedicated to Anne.

1

Watching for God

THERE is a story, which is only a story, told about an orphanage, where the regime was very strict. One of the orphans, a boy of ten, had a longing to watch the sun rise at dawn over the lake in the grounds, but the rules forbade any child from getting up and leaving the dormitory before the bell rang in the morning. One day, however, he wakes early and, guessing that dawn is close, takes his courage in his hands. He gets up, dresses, and tiptoes out of the dormitory, down the corridor, and out into the garden. As dawn breaks, he is entranced by the beauty of the sun rising over the water of the lake. For a while, he loses all sense of time. Then he comes to and realizes that it is late and the others will be getting up; his adventure will be discovered and he will be punished. He turns to go in, but then turns back and speaks to the lake: 'I'll go back now. Thank you. I don't care if I'm punished. Because I know something now – I know that the God of the lake is greater than the God of the orphanage.'

Michael Paul Gallagher tells this story in his book, *Where is your God?*,[1] to contrast different images of God, severe or beautiful, legalistic or loving. My purpose, although related, is a little different. The story also illustrates that people may discover God in a variety of ways, for example, by reading the Scriptures or listening to the teaching of the Church, through friendship or, as here, by gazing on the beauties of nature. There is plenty of evidence that the experience of conversion has taken many people by surprise. But then as the suspicion of God's existence dawns on us, or faith in God takes hold of us, or our relationship with God develops, one particular quality is needed. The boy at dawn, gazing out over the lake, illustrates it. It is watchfulness. We must be on the watch for God's presence. John Henry Newman, that remarkable nineteenth-century churchman whose life and writings have had such a significant influence on so many people, once described watchfulness as 'the very definition of a Christian'.[2] Like that child, we need to be on the alert for God's presence, expectant, perceptive.

This perceptiveness is an attitude, a cast of mind, a whole way of looking at things. It is not developed in isolation, but nurtured by the very God for whom it watches. What we see and how we see have an influence on each other. Those who believe see more. Newman once told his future biographer, Wilfrid Ward, that 'there *must* be more grounds in reason to a religious mind . . . in fact a religious mind must always master much which is unsure to the non-religious'. The idea may seem tortuous. In his biography, Ward paraphrased these remarks, but as a direct quotation: 'The religious mind sees much which is invisible to the irreligious mind. They have not the same evidence before them.'[3] Stated so baldly, this view may seem like special pleading. It is not. It is rather a matter of recognizing that there is a perceptiveness appropriate to and necessary for religious faith, just as there is an ear needed to appreciate music and an eye for art.

Our Christian lives are lives of faith. They are a response to the mysteries which were revealed to us supremely in the person of Jesus of Nazareth who is the Christ. Exploring the mysteries of this personal revelation, we are drawn into deep truths, whose meaning we can never exhaust in this life. We can make a profession of this faith.

We believe in one God who created us out of love. And we believe that the one God is Father and Son and Holy Spirit. We believe that God who is Son was born in time as Jesus of Nazareth, an ordinary human being like any one of us, but as truly divine as he was human; the wonder of the incarnation is to be found in the union of his human ordinariness with his divinity. We believe that he was born for a reason: we human beings had rejected God's love for us; we call that rejection sin; but he came out of love for us to save us from our sins and reconcile us to the Father by revealing to us the depth and wonder of God's love for us: he made known this love by embracing its consequences without reserve, even to being crucified and dying on the cross; and we believe that on the third day he was seen by his disciples, risen from the dead. These appearances were not hallucinations, induced by grief or desire, but privileged experiences of his presence.

And we believe that shortly afterwards God the Holy Spirit came down on these disciples and that, through this divine indwelling, they became a community. We call it the Church, the body of Christ, the people of God. As such, they lived by sharing in the life of the Spirit, who endowed them with the spirit of Christ's life. This life is both interior and invisible and also outward, external, and visible. We believe that we are one with the disciples in the same Spirit and have been made so by particular acts, which we call sacraments. By baptism we are reborn in Christ; by confirmation we are consecrated for service; by the eucharist our new life is nourished; by reconciliation our sins are forgiven; when anointed, our sickness is united with the Lord's suffering; and in marriage and holy orders our discipleship finds expression. They are living signs and expressions of God's love for us. They make us full members of the Church and help to sustain us in it throughout our lives. And we believe that, if we have died in God's love, we will be raised to everlasting life.

Such beliefs we profess. The statement may seem stark and compressed. But our faith is more than the conclusion to an intellectual exercise. We have to do more than hold certain views: we must act in ways which bear witness to this mystery of Christ and reflect the deep truths in which we believe; in other words, our beliefs must influence our behaviour, they give rise to a moral vision. Our lives, moreover, should be marked by other qualities, most notably the strength of our faith, the unreserved generosity of our love, and our firm hope in

everlasting life. Incalculably beneficial to the Christian faith as
much philosophy across the centuries may have been, Christianity cannot be reduced to an abstract mental system. As faith
is a response, we must be on the watch. We must be on the
watch for Christ's presence so as to enter the mystery, to seek
out the deep truths, through him.

Some people who believe may find this talk of watchfulness
discouraging. If left unqualified, it may even start to undermine
their faith. Bewildered by religious difficulties, they may seem
to themselves lost in a dense fog. They do not recognize their
own watchfulness. They would deny any awareness of Christ's
presence; they would say they perceive nothing; and so they may
conclude that their faith has evaporated. Or they may decide it
never existed in the first place. It is necessary to proceed with
care.

It is important to remember that perceptiveness, watchfulness,
the eyes of faith – whatever expression may be used – is not
simply vision, a matter of clear sight. It is a cast of mind, a *way*
of looking. What we are looking for is profound, it is the
presence of Christ Jesus. It may often seem lost from view. There
can be dark times when it is hidden entirely. But we must remain
watchful, on the alert for any glimpse we can catch of the Christ
and the mysteries he reveals.

Essential to our perceiving is the *desire* to perceive, the longing
to know him and to enter into these mysteries with love. It is
an aspect to which we will return.[4] For the present, it is enough
to realize that we are not alone. The Spirit of God is active here,
helping us to understand the gifts bestowed on us by God.[5] We
must be on the watch for what has been revealed to us. This
need for watchfulness, for being perceptive is, of course, brought
before us at the start of each liturgical year, that is, in Advent.

(ii)

We are an Advent people. No other season captures so exactly
the real nature of the Christian condition as those few weeks

before Christmas, during which we prepare to celebrate the birth of Jesus. Superficially, it may seem rather disorientating. We are looking in three different directions at the same time: we are contemplating the present moment, but looking forward to the celebration of Christmas, which is a past event. In fact, the Advent season is a call to watchfulness. We turn to our past to take hold of it afresh: in the birth of Jesus, who was truly both divine and human, our true dignity is revealed; we look to the future: we remind ourselves to be on the watch for his coming in glory; and we contemplate the present to discern his abiding presence in our midst. Advent draws together our past, our present, and our future, and its essential mark is watchfulness. Yet watchfulness is not a characteristic confined to Advent. It needs to become a feature which permeates our entire lives. We need to be on the watch from the beginning, like the boy in the orphanage. Indeed, it is a quality which we associate naturally with that childlikeness which Jesus commended to his disciples.

You will remember the scene which the evangelists narrate. Matthew, Mark, and Luke all speak of people bringing children to Jesus 'that he might touch them'. The disciples try to prevent them, but are rebuked. Jesus tells them, 'Let the children come to me, do not hinder them; for to such belongs the kingdom of God. Truly, I say to you, whoever does not receive the kingdom of God like a child shall not enter it.'[6] Matthew's Gospel, more-over, contains words by which Jesus settles a dispute among his disciples when they were quarrelling over their status in the kingdom: 'Truly, I say to you, unless you turn and become like children, you will never enter the kingdom of heaven.'[7] It is a stock-in-trade of preachers to point out the distinction between childlikeness and childishness, but we need to take seriously for ourselves that perceptiveness which comes to children in-stinctively and safeguard it as we grow older. Examples of it come readily to mind.

One of my treasured possessions for more than thirty years has been a set of responses collated from some essays written by thirteen-year-olds in 1968, who had been asked to write on what they thought a priest should be like. Their comments make fascinating reading. They are direct and clear. At times, their expectations are overwhelming, as, for example, when they require a priest to know enough about religion 'to be able to answer any questions about it', but the nub of the point – that priests need to be knowledgeable – is beyond dispute. Time and again, they strike gold.

They stress the importance of a priest being able to understand the problems of the day, of his helping people in their troubles, 'like Christ used to do when he lived on earth', of his being holy, 'but not too pious', and sociable, kind, sympathetic, gentle, and responsible for people. They show an awareness of a priest's limitations, especially when preaching sermons: 'Some priests are very nervous and they don't know what to say, but they shouldn't be, because they are just like us.' There are insights into pastoral practice: 'He should be kind and helpful to everyone, even if he doesn't like them very much.' Again, he 'should be kind and thoughtful. He should always be happy and smiling . . . he ought to be stern, but not too stern with the younger people . . . but not too soft.' The emphasis on being happy and smiling recurred frequently. It was linked with being normal. One said: 'The priest should be happy and join in with the happenings around and about his parish; he should not only be happy, but let others see that he is happy.' And another declared, 'He should be very happy, because there is no point in getting unhappy about religion.' Again, he 'should be as normal as any human being'. And another remarked, 'He should be normal more or less' – which is a nice touch; and then, this being 1968, added, 'He should not spend all his life in church. He should go to the pictures and smoke, and not everywhere he goes give a sermon.' There is much more, about having fun, going on holidays, and not living 'like a holy statue'. All in all, these observations reveal a remarkable grasp of essentials, combined with the conviction that non-essentials are not worth bothering about. The perceptiveness of these young people is evident all the time. Here is childlikeness.

Another example occurred when I was preaching once on this very subject. I must have been making fairly heavy weather of it. I learnt later that one young girl in the congregation had turned to her father and asked, 'Does he mean that children sometimes understand things which grown-ups miss?' Her question not only went to the point; it illustrated it as well. We need this quality, this perceptiveness. We must be on the watch to enter more deeply into the mysteries, the deep truths in which we believe. But there is more to it than that. We must not only become perceptive, watchful people ourselves; the way we live our Christian lives ought to encourage and evoke that perceptiveness in others.

(iii)

In his autobiography, *Blessings in Disguise*, Sir Alec Guinness recalls an incident which took place during the filming of *Father Brown* on location in Burgundy. Late one afternoon he had walked the three kilometres or so from his hotel to the set in a small hilltop village. He discovered, however, that he would not be needed for several hours and so decided to return to his room. Dressed as a priest, he began the walk back. 'By now,' he says, 'it was dark.' He continues:

> I hadn't gone far when I heard scampering footsteps and a piping voice calling, 'Mon père!' My hand was seized by a boy of seven or eight, who clutched it tightly, swung it and kept up a non-stop prattle. He was full of excitement, hops, skips and jumps, but never let go of me. I didn't dare speak in case my excruciating French should scare him. Although I was a total stranger he obviously took me for a priest and so to be trusted. Suddenly with a 'Bonsoir, mon père', and a hurried sideways sort of bow, he disappeared through a hole in a hedge. He had had a happy, reassuring

walk home, and I was left with an odd calm sense of elation. Continuing my walk I reflected that a Church which could inspire such confidence in a child, making its priests, even when unknown, so easily approachable could not be as scheming and creepy as so often made out.[8]

We have learnt more recently that there have been occasions when such childlikeness has been betrayed. Our times have become less innocent. But the incident is instructive. Guinness says that through it he 'began to shake off my long-taught, long-absorbed prejudices' against the Catholic Church. At first it might be said that this child was anything but perceptive: he identified as a real priest an actor dressed up to look like one. But on further reflection it bears clear witness to the kind of experience of the Church and its priests which that child had had, one that inspired ease, friendliness, and confidence, directness and simplicity. The child was just being a child. But he served the gospel: he nudged an actor towards faith. We need to become people whose alertness to Christ's presence can stir that perceptiveness in others.

This watchfulness may be cultivated more readily when allied with a sense of urgency.

(iv)

There is perhaps no passage in the Gospels which brings home this element of urgency so well as St Mark's account of the healing of the blind beggar, Bartimaeus, who forced himself on Jesus as he was leaving Jericho with his disciples.[9] The story, which will be familiar to many, was brought alive for me long ago by Metropolitan Anthony of Sourozh.[10] Let me try to follow his example by fleshing it out for you in a similar way.

I like to imagine Bartimaeus begging on the outskirts of Jericho, listening to the gossip each day and learning about a new wandering teacher, Jesus from Nazareth, who was travelling through the country, preaching and doing good, and who was reputed to have performed wonders. 'Like what?' Bartimaeus may have asked and been told of lepers cleansed, the lame who walked again, and the deaf with their hearing restored. All well and good, Bartimaeus must have thought, but the vital question for him was: 'Had he ever made a blind man see?' Who knows what he would have been told? Perhaps they answered no, but added that the occasion had never arisen; perhaps they said yes, they had heard of such a report. In either case, Bartimaeus must have been torn by mixed emotions; on the one hand, the hope that a cure could be found for him through the power of this man Jesus and, on the other, his sadness at the impossibility for him, a blind man, of ever finding and meeting Jesus. Was he ever likely to come to Jericho? Could he allow himself that hope? The remote chance of a cure may have made its lack all the harder to bear.

Then one day, as he crouches begging under the city wall, he detects – in the way that people can when one sense is disabled – a change in the noise made by the crowd milling about him. He cannot see them, but he hears the difference, the stir of excitement. He asks what is going on and learns that Jesus of Nazareth is near. Imagine his emotion now. The longed-for, unexpected opportunity has come. Jesus is present. Present, but passing. In Metropolitan Anthony's words, 'every step was bringing him nearer and nearer, and then every step would take him farther and farther away'.[11] Bartimaeus' delight at the opportunity is mingled with an urgency to seize the moment, lest it pass never to return. And so he cries out, 'Jesus, Son of David, have mercy on me!' The crowds are at once irritated by his shouts and tell him to be quiet. But he is gripped with urgency and cries out all the more. Jesus hears him and calls for him. The mood of the crowd changes. Jesus' attention makes them encourage him. 'Take heart;' they say, 'rise, he is calling you.' Bartimaeus springs up and hears the question, 'What do you want me to do for you?' And he answers, 'Master, let me receive my sight.' And we are told, 'And Jesus said to him, "Go your way; your faith has made you well." And immediately he received his sight and followed him on the way.'

God's love for us is constant; it will never fail. God is always present to us in Christ and will never desert us. We know that in theory, but need to take hold of it in practice. Although the presence is a constant, abiding presence, it can also be hidden. We need to be alert, on the watch, for those graced moments in which it is unveiled for us. It is possible to miss them. The love of a particular person, a visit to a particular place, some crisis which may bring either happiness or tragedy, even the reading of a particular book – possibly this one – may be the occasion when the reality of that presence and love breaks in on us. So we need to be on the watch for it, perceptive in order to recognize it, should it be disclosed to us. Remember St Christopher.

The popular legend tells how Christopher was assigned to help travellers ford a river and how one day a child whom he carried across revealed himself as the Child Jesus. The story is familiar. Its origins in any actual event are lost in the distant past, but its power as a parable may move us still. And so I like to imagine Christopher engaged in his given duty, carrying people to and fro, until one day indeed a child asks to be ferried to the other side. The child was any child, but Christopher suddenly to his surprise recognizes in this child the presence of Christ. To carry this child across the stream was to carry Christ. And after that every person whom he assisted, child or adult, young or old, woman or man, was someone in whom he recognized that presence. That is the perceptiveness we all need, so as to see in the ordinary circumstances of our lives each day, in people and places and events and within ourselves also, the unyielding reality of God's love for us and his abiding presence in Christ. Such perceptiveness flows from what the psalmist calls 'a heart of wisdom'.[12] It is nurtured in prayer.

2

Prayer

(i)

WHEN I was at school more than forty years ago, three days used to be set aside at the beginning of each academic year for a retreat. They were days for silence and reflection which a visiting priest would direct through a series of talks. On at least two occasions our director was Fr Patrick Rorke, who died in 1990.[1] Later we became friends. As a boy, I just saw a wise, gentle giant. It was hard to realize that he had been released from a Japanese prisoner of war camp a mere thirteen or so years before.

I learnt a number of valuable lessons from Pat Rorke over the years, but one remark from those early meetings stands out clearly. I remember him turning to our group one morning and saying, 'I could give this whole retreat on prayer.' Just as clearly I can recall my own relief that he was going to confine himself to the single forty-five minute session. That was quite enough in my view. Talks about prayer were boring.

Some years later my studies for the priesthood began. The bell used to ring at 5.25 in the morning and we had to be in chapel by 6.00 for a half-hour of silent prayer before the community mass at 6.30. This daily routine and the experience which dawned with it uncovered for me little by little what Pat Rorke could have meant. I came to understand gradually the value of prayer and its importance. Before going any further, it might be useful to set down some of the points which have guided me and which might also be helpful for others. Prayer nurtures our perceptiveness for God. We want to pray well. But what does it mean, to pray well?

(ii)

Many people nowadays take prayer seriously, but at the same time are anxious because they are convinced that they pray badly. When questioned, they explain that they are often distracted, feel flat and empty, and in any case cannot find the words they want. They know that prayer is important, but often feel bored and, therefore, guilty. They seem to receive little comfort from their praying and become discouraged. Surely communing with God ought to be wonderful; as it is not, they blame themselves. Their prayer, they conclude, is very poor.

In these circumstances, it can be worth asking how it ought to be. What would good prayer be like?

According to this view, it would presumably be in stark contrast to the experience described. It would be full of interest, free of distraction, eloquent, and accompanied by a consoling sense of ease and contentment. Are those really the marks of good prayer? When we are, as we may say, praying well, what do we suppose is happening? In my more comfortable, eloquent moments of prayer, is Almighty God astounded by my depth and eloquence? Is he sitting on his triune throne and turning to the choirs of angels to remark, 'What a fascinating idea Rod Strange has had this morning! I'd never thought of it like that before.' Cast in those terms, the absurdity of the notion is apparent at once. The quality of our prayer cannot be judged so easily.

The fundamental truth about prayer and praying is its utter simplicity. But this simplicity, however, needs to be understood properly. What is simple is not necessarily easy. Think of some cartoons. I think of Calman's political cartoons in *The Times*. They were no more than a few lines, but those few lines said so much. They made a point, they made you think, they made you laugh. The skill lay in the simplicity. If simple meant easy, everyone could produce such cartoons. Few can. What is simple is not complex, but it may be difficult. Prayer is simple and we often find it very difficult indeed. The key to its simplicity is desire. It does not depend on how we feel. We have to make a decision. That is what makes it simple. Prayer is not a complex operation. To pray we need only to wish to pray. Praying is a matter of longing to come close to God. This longing is not based on emotion, but decision. We want to come close to God. In the familiar phrase, it is the raising of the mind and heart to God. There is no need to become entangled in specialist techniques. Anyone can do it. If we want to come close to God – or even if we wish we did, which at times of discouragement may be as much as we can manage – then that desire itself is prayer. In the words of Sr Wendy Mary Beckett, 'Prayer is prayer if we want it to be.'[2] Her account is outstanding for its brevity, clarity, and power.

'Prayer is prayer if we want it to be.' Does that seem too easy? In a way it is easy and not so far removed from our common experience as we might at first suppose. Let me explain.

Some years ago, on a day visit to London from the Northwest for a meeting, I took the opportunity to meet a friend for a bite of supper before taking the train home. We had not met for some time. But it was all rather rushed and I felt fairly tired from travelling and the earlier business of the day. Although I was delighted we could get together, our meal was not a notably sparkling occasion. I felt too weary to be good company. As we said goodbye, I said how sorry I was not to have been on better form. My friend would hear nothing of it. 'What's important,' she said, 'is that you wanted us to meet.' And she thanked me for getting in touch. And I was left thinking how right she was. When friends meet, it is not simply for fascinating conversation, hilarious jokes, or the latest news, marvellous as all that might be. What matters most is the fact that they wanted to meet. The wish, the desire, to meet is crucial. Many people, I am sure, can tell a similar story. And if that is true for us, if friends welcome each other because they have wanted to meet, will not God also welcome us when we approach him, however stumbling our steps, dulled our emotions, and garbled our words may be, if only we long to come close to him? It is the desire for intimacy with God which makes our praying prayer. It is as simple as that.

It is simple, but it can also be hard to do. This direct approach leaves us exposed. We are placing ourselves in the hands of the living God. It is so much more reassuring to ponder over some spiritual work, whether a classic or the latest bestseller, so much easier to share pious insights in a prayerful manner with a group, so much safer to seek counsel from a wise and trusted director. Do not misunderstand me. There is a time and place for all these activities, the spiritual reading, the prayer group, spiritual direction, but we need to be aware of how we are using them so as not to misuse them by making them a shield behind which we can take shelter from the divine presence. Prayer is simple, but it can make us fearful, for it brings us close to God, naked and unprotected, vulnerable, exposed, and in his control. For many of us daily survival involves a degree of posturing; we put on a bit of an act. There is no place for that in prayer. To quote Wendy Beckett again, 'The essential act of prayer is to stand unprotected before God.' And she asks, 'What will God do?' And she supplies the answer, 'He will take possession of us.'[3] It is not surprising if we find the prospect alarming.

Most people who read a book like this will be the kind who have their lives under control. Presented with a problem, they grapple with it and resolve it. That is their instinctive response. It is a consequence of their education, an indication of their professionalism. I recognize the same tendency in myself. Yet one of the lessons I have learnt, particularly from reading Jock Dalrymple, that remarkable Edinburgh priest who died in 1985, has been the need to reverse this instinct in prayer. Prayer is not a problem to be solved by our mastering God, but a condition in which God masters us. As Dalrymple says, 'We have to "change gear" at the beginning of prayer and deliberately let drop all desire to be in charge, to know where we are going, to master the situation.'[4] We have to learn to be receptive and so allow God to pour his love into us. He will not impose himself. Once again, perceptiveness is vital. We need to be on the alert for this loving presence so as to welcome him into our hearts, into the very core of our being.

(iii)

Prayer is simple. There is no complex science, no maze of techniques. It is not a method for learning about God. We must long for him simply, come close to him, free ourselves to be mastered by him, and be drawn into his presence so as to be possessed by him. Desire is the key. God is present every-where, but in prayer we are attentive to that presence. Prayer is the turning to the presence. There are old books of meditations which always make me smile. They consist mainly of themes, drawn up under three headings. What brings the smile is the way, at the beginning of each theme, we are told to place ourselves in the presence of God; and then we read in brackets, '(2 mins.)'. We know, of course, what is meant; we are being invited to compose ourselves for prayer; but if only that simple instruction could be perfectly fulfilled, we would be wrapped in the utter stillness of that presence and we would wish for nothing more.

When we seek God's presence, however, we do not necessarily become aware of it automatically. It is true that there may be times when our desire for God is matched by a sense of his presence. When our desire and that emotion are at one, they bring us comfort, strength, encouragement, and consolation. They are blessed times. But such experiences are not common, and so we need to have confidence in God's abiding presence; we must not become disillusioned when, in spite of desire, there seems to be only emptiness. There may be periods when God seems to be absent. In those circumstances various conclusions can be drawn.

I think of the boy Samuel in the temple. One night, at a time, according to the Scriptures, when people rarely heard God's word or saw visions, Samuel, who was serving the priest Eli, was wakened by a voice, calling him, 'Samuel, Samuel'. He got

up and naturally went to Eli. 'Here I am, for you called me,' he
said; but Eli denied it and told him to go back and lie down.
The call came again and Samuel got up; again the old man sent
him back. The call came a third time; but on this occasion,
when he sent him back to lie down, Eli gave him a word of
advice, for, we are told, he 'perceived that the Lord was calling
the boy'. So he added, 'if he calls you, you shall say, "Speak,
Lord, for your servant is listening." ' And the call came again
and Samuel answered, 'Speak, for your servant is listening'; and
the Lord spoke to Samuel.[5]

What is noteworthy for us about this incident is the fact that
God has called to Samuel three times without his recognizing
him. It may prompt us to wonder how often he has called to us
without our realizing it. When God seems far removed, is he
really absent or are we being inattentive to the way in which
he is present? He may not come in a way we would presume or
expect. Eli perceived the presence, but Samuel at first did not.
Are we being insensitive to that presence? Do we perhaps assume
that it must take some conventional form?

We need to be alert to the possibility of that presence in other
people, in nature, in art, in literature, in light and in darkness,
and so forth. There is no need to lapse into sentimentality. It is
not a question simply of stirring up feeling artificially, but of a
keener sensitivity to the divine presence. It is a matter once again
of perceptiveness.

At the same time, if God seems to be absent from us, our
inattention is not the only possible explanation. While we have
to be alert for the ways in which he is present, ways which we
may not expect and which may take us by surprise, it is also
true that there are dark times when we search, but are confronted
only by absence. The mystics speak of the dark night of the
senses and the dark night of the spirit. It is, of course, only
common sense for us not to identify every period of discourage-
ment with profound mystical experiences of trial, but it would
also be wise not to regard such experiences as so lofty that they

are confined to an élite and, as such, utterly beyond us. It is
not so.

Most people who want prayer to be a constant and vital part
of their lives, will strike hard, dry patches, when their praying
is a time of struggle, drudgery, and tedium. They have not been
using prayer for emotional solace, as an escape; they have
been content to put up with its dullness, a dullness characteristic
of any routine; but they have never expected to be so disenchanted by it, to find it so utterly unrewarding, so completely
lacking in comfort. They do not give up. They carry on praying,
but it is an altogether thankless task. Only their faith sustains
them. And later they emerge from their ordeal, restored. What
had comforted them before, perhaps the liturgy or group prayer,
is viewed now in a fresh way, because this loss of consolation
has challenged them. Now they come before God more directly.
Their participation in liturgy or involvement in the group has
been renewed. They have been purified. They have undergone
a dark night of the senses.

There are others, however, from whom even the support of
faith is removed. Stripped of all sensible comfort, they suddenly
wonder whether they even believe. This is the dark night of the
spirit and many people, who make no claim to being special,
will be able to recognize it. It has been described acutely by
Jock Dalrymple:

> This second Dark Night is considerably more disturbing
> and painful than the earlier surface one, since it threatens
> us at the root of all we believe in and all we stand for.
> There is not much that can be said about it, since words
> are not much use here. A detached observer can explain
> that this experience is God's way of strengthening our faith,
> by the paradoxical way of threatening to destroy it, so that
> we have to exercise it more than ever before. Our reaction
> to the night and the darkness in the depth of our being
> is to make renewed, 'blind', acts of faith and trust in God.
> A book like this can comment clinically on God's design,

but the experience itself is far from detached. You cannot say to yourself: this is God's design, all is well, because you are in the process of doubting whether God exists and whether there is such a design. Christianity appears to be a fairy tale, with any number of psychological explanations. You feel you have deceived yourself about God and about prayer, that any experiences you may have had in the past were self-induced, perhaps escape mechanisms to justify not getting involved in the world of action. The whole 'God business' appears a hollow sham. Yet you plod on in bewilderment, believing against belief, hoping against hope. The reward, when it is all over, is strengthened faith and hope, strengthened christian purpose.[6]

In all circumstances, often light, but sometimes dark, we must cling to the reality of the divine presence abiding with us.

We are trying to become people of that simple prayer which is marked by a longing for God and a sensitivity to his presence. This very simplicity can be daunting. To ward off discouragement, we can usefully bear a number of practical points in mind.

(iv)

'Pray as you can and do not try to pray as you can't'
Dom John Chapman, who was Abbot of Downside from 1929 to 1933, used to offer this advice and it is an invaluable way to begin.[7] When we start to pray seriously on our own, there is a real danger that we will go in search of some ideal, right way to pray. It does not exist. We have rather to discover the way of praying which is natural to us and not strain after a style which is alien and so which for us can never be prayer. There are many possibilities available. We can kneel or sit, stand or walk about; some will gaze at a crucifix, a statue, or a picture; others will close their eyes, or find a darkened room; some will recite familiar, favourite prayers; others will use brief phrases like 'My Lord and my God', or 'Into your hands I commend my spirit',

while others again will read from Scripture, and yet others will lapse into silence. These variations are not exhaustive. It is important for each of us to discover which style we find most helpful and to remember as well that that style is not carved in stone: it will change. There will be times for speaking and times for silence. Many adults have diagnosed their spiritual lives as moribund only because they have failed to recognize that they are committed to forms of praying which may have been appropriate in the past, but which they have outgrown. They are not so much sick, as suffering from arrested development.

Silence

There are times for speaking and times for silence. Some people will be attracted to silence, while others will never abandon words altogether; nor perhaps should they; but silence of another kind is indispensable. We need an inner silence, for our prayer is not only a matter of our addressing God; we must learn to listen as well. True watchfulness will require it. We have to be attentive. How else can we know in our place what St Ignatius of Antioch on his way to martyrdom expressed with such power and clarity? He told the Romans, 'Earthly longings have been crucified; in me there is left no spark of desire for mundane things, but only a murmur of living water that whispers within me, "Come to the Father".'[8] Such perception is unlikely to occur without stillness within. We need silence, but it is hard to find. We must take time to create it.

Time

To mention finding time can cause irritation. It is all very well for the clergy, people say, to urge us to find time for prayer, but they will not have been up nursing babies through the night and getting the older children off to school first thing in the morning before going out to work. And many of them will not be cooking on their return. The laity simply do not have spare time available like that; it is a clerical luxury. The view of a priest's life implicit in this reaction is not entirely accurate, but we can leave that question aside. What is true is the fact that for many of us time is in short supply. I have beside me a letter from a friend, a wife and mother of five. She writes, 'It's also difficult to find settled times when I can pray, although I do manage to have a time each day to be alone and quiet. I try to read the mass readings and prayers for the day and to reflect for a while, and remove myself from all the frenetic rush of children and household duties. It's not easy, even though the family are more independent now.'[9] What struck me on reading this letter was how, amidst all the difficulties, she was still trying to carve out that bit of time. And it is also true that most of us can find time for something if we want to do it enough.

I remember as a university chaplain in Oxford looking out of my window in the early morning. Even in miserable weather, the shadowy figures of undergraduates could be seen running through the rain and mist to train for an hour or more, rowing on the Cherwell. Then there were others, not studying music, who would nevertheless find long hours to practise the piano or violin or some other instrument, or to sing in choirs, or to act in plays. The list could be extended. These, of course, were students, but they were not idle; indeed, the hardest working were notable for the way they made time for so many interests. That seems to be the general rule: the busiest people can find the extra time. I know other people as well whose days have been kidnapped virtually completely by their responsibilities, but they are the exceptions – and, indeed, they too tend to find some time and space for themselves. They have to. However, most of us can protect at least a small part of each day, or at least each week, even if it is only fifteen minutes or half-an-hour, for some activity, if we value it enough. If we want to pray, we will find the time.

Time is important and necessary, because it helps us become familiar with prayer. Praying does not come naturally to most of us. In fact, learning to pray may be compared to learning a foreign language. The same rules apply. Occasional bursts of enthusiasm will not make much difference, but regular, steady application can gradually make a way of speaking which is alien to us become natural, so that in time we will be speaking like a native. Prayer is the native language of God's country. If we will give time to it seriously, not giving up because we feel a bit bored nor exhausting our efforts by excessive enthusiasm, we will find not only that it is a language we can speak, but even one we can use as fluently as our own.

Such seriousness in practice will mean fixing the time we will give to prayer. Once that has been settled, it is important that we stick to it. We should not cut it short, however unrewarding it may seem, nor lengthen it, either to compensate for distractions or even – and this advice may seem surprising – or even when carried away with its delight. It will be enough to give that chosen time faithfully each day.

Habit

If we are faithful to our time of prayer, it will become habitual. It may remain in part a struggle; there may always be the lurking temptation to spend the time in some other way; but once the habit is established, it becomes difficult to break. More than thirty years ago, I heard Fr Michael Hollings, one of my most distinguished predecessors at the Oxford chaplaincy, catch the point in a way that has often helped me since. 'Prayer,' he remarked, 'is addictive, but the hangover comes first.' We can usually find excuses for not praying, but, once we are committed to it and the habit is formed, we will find ourselves drawn to pray, irrespective of our feelings, because our feelings – whether enthusiastic or bored – will no longer be controlling our behaviour. Desire is the key. Praying will have become an integral part of our lives. It will put our distractions into perspective as well.

Distractions

Distractions can cause us worry quite unnecessarily. We really ought not to bother about them too much. Of course, there may be occasions which we set aside for prayer, but then spend the time quite deliberately absorbed in something else, perhaps planning a party for the weekend. In those circumstances, we are not praying at all, or probably not. Most distractions, however, are not deliberate. They come from the imagination which is the least disciplined part of our minds. If we settle down to pray at the end of a busy day, it is not to be expected that the imagination, which will have been active for hours, will suddenly go calm. Once again, we must remember that it is the will which takes priority, the longing for God which is the essential part of our praying. Abbot Chapman used to strike a relaxed, balanced note: 'When the will fixes itself on God, and leaves the imagination entirely to itself, the latter flies off into any absurdity. Provided these imaginations are not *wilful* they don't matter in the least.'[10] The will is vital, our desire to come close to God.

All the same, our distractions may be instructive. It can be helpful to glance at them from time to time. Why was the planning for that weekend party so absorbing? Perhaps it was indicating to us what we really care about.

We have noticed already the danger of idealizing one particular kind of prayer. We need rather to know what concerns us most. Our distractions, like planning that party, may be embarrassingly trivial, but then perhaps in some ways so are we. I do not mean it insultingly. However, it may be that our distractions show us who we really are, not people, cloaked in the grandeur of perfection, but little people, weak, inadequate, often superficial. Our distractions can be valuable, because they reveal us to ourselves. Such knowledge is priceless. That is where our praying must begin: with our real selves, not the person we would ideally like to be. When we start there, we may discover that we no longer fall victim to distractions so easily, because we will be praying about what matters to us: to echo the teaching of Victor White, passed on by Fr Herbert McCabe, 'the prayers of people on sinking ships are rarely troubled by distractions'.[11] Our longing for God will no longer be obscured by our delusions.

Conclusion

It would be possible to continue this sequence of practical points for some time, but these five may be sufficient at the start to encourage us to begin. They offer us confidence in ourselves as people capable of prayer. By finding and following our own style and by listening patiently, habitually, and in spite of distractions, we will discover that our capacity for prayer is in fact a gift from God, for it is not something which, first of all, we do. We do not take the initiative. It is something God does in us. 'God thirsts that we may thirst for him.'[12] God prays in us, the Father drawing us into communion with the Son. We become people of prayer. We pray constantly.

(v)

St Paul told the Thessalonians to pray constantly. It is a most improbable command. It comes as one of a series of abrupt orders: 'admonish the idlers, encourage the fainthearted, help the weak', and then, shortly afterwards, 'pray constantly.'[13] These instructions may be understood most naturally as ways of preparing for the Lord's second coming. It was thought to be imminent: the community was well advised to give itself over to constant prayer. But now the perspective on that second coming has shifted, we may ask what meaning it has for us. Does it have any meaning at all? We have considered already the fact that we are an Advent people, on the watch for Christ and his coming. Yet how are we to fulfil realistically this command to pray constantly? We cannot be for ever murmuring formal prayers. That would make no sense. We need to uncover the significance of Paul's words, interpret them afresh. I find it helpful to explore the distinction between a rehearsal and a performance.

Imagine a pianist, rehearsing a Chopin sonata for hours in order to perfect her performance of it. Were she to neglect to do so, her performance would certainly suffer, her interpretation would be weak or superficial, her technique clumsy and flawed.

Rehearsals are vital. All the same, there is no question that it is the performance that matters. There would be something unbearably sad about a pianist who rehearsed obsessively, but was always dissatisfied with her standard and so never agreed to perform. When we think about prayer and our lives, then it is our lives that matter: they, so to speak, are the performance. To make them truly lives of prayer, however, we must also rehearse.

The times we give to prayer prepare us. They are our rehearsals. To call them that is not meant to diminish their significance; it is wonderful to be rapt in longing for God; but the image of rehearsal is a way of illustrating the relationship between that time spent in prayer and the rest of our lives. The times offered to God, simply and directly, longing for him, listening to him, day by day, have their influence upon us. They form us as people whose every moment can be prayerful. And the wonder of it is that the ratio of rehearsal to performance is reversed. While a musician will rehearse for hours and hours daily in order to perform a piece which may last no more than fifteen or twenty minutes, if we will pray daily for fifteen or twenty minutes, we can transform the rest of our lives. It will not happen all at once; it may never happen perfectly in this life; but it does happen. Gradually our lives are taken over by prayerfulness, possessed by the divine presence, so that everything we do wells up from this reality deep within us. It is a condition like love; indeed, it is a condition of love. We are not absorbed with thoughts of the beloved all the time: that may occur in young romantic love. But as love deepens and becomes more mysterious, the beloved's presence becomes more real, though often subconscious, and it exercises its influence almost unawares. In a similar way, our praying will not amount to the constant uttering of prayers, but will flow more and more from the divine presence, secure within us.

Once we recognize God's presence as the source of our praying, once we realize that our praying flows from his praying within us, we discover not only that we can pray constantly, but we also understand better a problem that often troubles people. We wonder about those prayers which seem to go unanswered.

(vi)

We have been told, 'Ask, and it will be given you.'[14] And so we ask and sometimes it is given to us, but on other occasions it is not. We do not receive. We are perplexed at first, but then by chance we may come across the teaching of St James: 'You ask and do not receive, because you ask wrongly, to spend it on your passions.'[15] That makes matters worse. The lack of response to our prayer seems to charge it with insincerity. We had not meant it to be so, but that is the conclusion we are given. We feel guilty. Those whom we have wished to help through our prayers have been left as they were before, and it seems that our poor prayer is to blame. Is that really what we are being told? We should look more closely.

It is always a mistake to interpret a phrase in isolation. This text is a good example. James is not sowing scruples, trying to make good people anxious when they are praying sincerely, because the outcome is not what they had hoped for. He is instructing those whose requests in prayer are in fact inspired by bad motives, their selfishness and infidelity, to change their ways. Those are the attitudes, he says, which have handicapped their prayer. He urges them instead to submit themselves to God and uses words that match perfectly what has emerged in this chapter: 'Draw near to God and he will draw near to you.'[16] It has been our constant refrain that the heart of prayer is the simple longing for God, the desire to be in his presence so that his presence may come to fruition in us. Accordingly, all our prayers seek ultimately the fulfilment of the divine will. At the deepest point we always ask, 'Thy will be done.'

This deep underlying desire, however, may seem to be evasive, a trick-saving device. It is as though every request in prayer involves two elements: our immediate wish and the fulfilment of God's will. Then, if our immediate request goes unanswered, it can still be claimed that nevertheless God's will has been satisfied. Thus, it can be argued, our prayer has been answered, but not in the way we had hoped. And God's effectiveness has been safeguarded, because whatever happens is identified as the desired answer to prayer, because whatever happens is identified as God's will. It will not do. There must be more to prayer in accordance with the divine will than that.

What is happening when we petition God in prayer, if we are always praying, 'Thy will be done'?

The start of a solution to this question can perhaps be found by thinking first of the alternative. The alternative would be a prayer designed not to fulfil, but rather to frustrate, the divine will. We would be praying that God's will would *not* be done. Its petition would presumably begin, 'Lord God, contrary to your better judgement . . .', but we have only to utter the phrase to realize that it is nonsense, the invoking of a lesser good. All our praying must be rooted in our longing for God's will to be done. We do not pray to make God change his mind. That is the second point to grasp. When I pray for my friend in her early fifties, who has been fighting cancer for years, but now seems to be losing the battle, I am not tugging at God's sleeve to remind him of her. He has not forgotten her. Still less has he given her the illness. Cancer comes as part of the human condition, attacking some and leaving others. God holds her unfailingly in his love. And I pray, hoping that her pain may disappear, that she may enjoy some respite, that she may be cured, and I pray, hoping that that may be God's will for her and, by my prayer, I share in the fulfilment of that will. If it is not so, I shall not mourn any the less; I shall long for it to have been otherwise; but in the midst of bleak grief I hope I shall have the faith to bow my head and still say, 'Thy will be done.' Our prayers of petition are offered in hope and for a purpose, but always in accordance with God's will and as a way of taking our part in his care for us.[17]

We must long for God's presence in simplicity of heart and pray that God's will may be done. These aims should take possession of our lives, as they took possession of the life of Jesus. We can learn from him.

3

Jesus at Prayer

(i)

WHEN Jesus began his public ministry in Galilee, his reputation as a teacher and healer spread rapidly. Mark and Luke record a day early on, during which he taught at the synagogue in Capernaum with such authority that people were amazed, visited Simon's house and cured his mother-in-law of a fever, and then spent the evening healing the sick who were brought to him and casting out demons.[1] We are then told by Mark: 'And in the morning, a great while before day, he rose and went to a lonely place, and there he prayed.'[2] Anyone who has followed his example there by the Sea of Galilee at sunrise, will understand this action readily enough: it is a setting which inspires prayer. Later, in Luke's Gospel, before naming the twelve apostles, we learn that Jesus 'went out to the mountain to pray; and all night he continued in prayer to God'.[3] Again, after feeding the five thousand, he sent his disciples on ahead of him by boat, while he dismissed the crowds, 'And after he had taken leave of them, he went up on the mountain to pray.'[4] These few passing references may indicate for us the way the ministry of Jesus was nurtured in prayer. Yet they tell only a part of the story.

We have realized already that saying prayers is only the expression of an aspect of our lives; it is not enough to recite the words alone, we have to become prayerful people. The longing for God and the desire to do his will which make up the very heart of prayer, must take possession of us, as they did of Jesus. They must pervade everything we do, just as they touched everything he did. The Gospels bear ample witness to their influence, but three scenes in particular may be said to reveal their presence. When he was tempted, transfigured, and during his agony, we are shown in a heightened way how Jesus' desire to fulfil the Father's will, which is the very definition of his ministry, was inseparable from his longing for the Father, which is the very heart of prayerfulness. When we see Jesus at prayer on these occasions, we not only discover how prayerfulness nurtured his ministry, but his inner life begins to be unveiled for us as well. We are able to see a little more clearly who he was.

(ii)

Jesus is tempted

Those moments in the Gospel when Jesus sought time to pray, indicate his love of solitude, but, so far as we know, the only extended period when he was alone took place at the very start of his public ministry. The Marcan account could scarcely be more brief. After his baptism, we are told, 'The Spirit immediately drove him out into the wilderness. And he was in the wilderness forty days, tempted by Satan; and he was with the wild beasts; and the angels ministered to him.'[5] We do not know how long Jesus was alone; the reference to forty days is not a measurement, but a sign of the special quality of that time. And in this solitude Jesus was tempted.

Temptation is very personal. It is not surprising that Jesus should have felt tested before he began his public ministry, nor that he might later have mentioned it to the Twelve, who were his close friends. That could be the source for these texts. What actually happened, however, we cannot say. The Gospels of Matthew and Luke have elaborated the bald statement in Mark for their own purposes. There is no need to be alarmed by that. Their accounts have much to teach us, once we recognize what they were trying to do. Once again, we have to be alert, perceptive. These texts are so familiar. We hear them read to us each Lent, usually on the first Sunday of the season. We are used to being told to follow the example of Jesus and resist temptation, as he did. It is a good lesson, but largely innocent of the wealth and depth of the Gospel message. These texts are saturated in the story of the Chosen People. Like great symphonies echoing earlier melodies, they echo earlier themes. Once we begin to pursue the connections, they come alive in unexpected, startling ways.

Consider, first of all, St Matthew's account. Throughout his Gospel Matthew was always concerned to show the links and connections between the past and Jesus, between the promise and its fulfilment. His infancy narratives give a clear example of this approach. The text is studded with quotations from the Old Testament to illustrate the way the word spoken by the prophets was being fulfilled.[6] John the Baptist is then introduced in the words of the prophet Isaiah as 'The voice of one crying in the wilderness: Prepare the way of the Lord, make his paths straight.'[7] And after that Jesus is baptized. Then immediately, we are told, he is led by the Spirit into the wilderness to be tempted. The approach does not change; Matthew continues to draw on the past.

Jesus' special time of solitude – forty days and forty nights – recalls the forty years spent by the people of Israel in the wilderness, during which they were tested. His temptations revisit their trials. Moreover, his fasting throughout that time is a reminder of Moses' encounter with God on the mountain, when he received the Law: 'When I went up the mountain to receive the tables of stone, the tables of the covenant which the Lord made with you, I remained on the mountain forty days and forty nights; I neither ate bread nor drank water.'[8] That is the backcloth.

More particularly, we need to remember the great teaching of the Book of Deuteronomy, the *Shema Israel*, 'Hear, O Israel: The Lord our God is one Lord; and you shall love the Lord your God with all your heart, and with all your soul, and with all your might.'[9] It is important to know what is meant by 'heart', and 'soul', and 'might'. They are not simply parts of the human anatomy. The early rabbis understood the 'heart' to refer to that

depth within a human being from which our decisive choices
for good or evil arise; the 'soul' meant life itself; and 'might'
referred to wealth, property, and other external possessions,
whatever else makes us who we are. The teaching, therefore, is
a summons to love God from the very roots of our being, with
our entire lives, and with everything else we may possess. It is a
call to total love. With this understanding clear in our minds,
let us turn now to the temptations of Jesus to see what Matthew
is saying to us.

'The tempter came and said to him, "If you are the Son of
God, command these stones to become loaves of bread." '[10] The
designation 'Son of God' marks Jesus as representative of the
people of Israel. What is the nub of the temptation? Is it to
resort to magic to satisfy his hunger? Nothing so trivial. The
temptation recalls the way the people long ago had complained
of hunger in the wilderness and had chosen to satisfy their
hunger rather than continue to trust in the Lord's love for them;
and the Lord, in response, had satisfied their hunger, but with a
bread they did not recognize, manna, as a sign to them that 'man
does not live by bread alone, but that man lives by everything
that proceeds out of the mouth of the Lord.'[11] These are the
words used by Jesus when he was tempted. He has made no
complaint; he has chosen to continue his fast. By resisting temptation, by this choice, he revealed his acceptance of the Father's
will for him. He loved him with all his heart.

Next, according to Matthew, the tempter took Jesus to the
pinnacle of the Temple. Once again, he is designated as the representative of the people: 'If you are the Son of God, throw
yourself down; for it is written, "He will give his angels charge
of you," and "On their hands they will bear you up, lest you
strike your foot against a stone." '[12] Beyond the immediate challenge, however, a deeper issue is at stake. Jesus was being tempted
to test the Father, as the people had been tempted to test the
Lord in the wilderness when they were thirsty.[13] A test implies
a doubt. When thirsty, as when hungry, the people's trust faltered. But Jesus had no doubt. He spurned the temptation,

echoing ancient teaching once more: 'You shall not tempt the Lord your God.'[14] Where the people failed, he stood firm. Jesus trusted the Father with his entire life. He loved him with all his soul.

The third temptation took place on the top of a very high mountain. The devil offered Jesus the kingdoms of the world and their glory, if he would worship him. Again, there is the echo of the people's trial in the wilderness, when they were tempted to idolatry and fashioned a golden calf. But Jesus dismissed the devil abruptly, 'Away with you, Satan!', and recalled the words of Deuteronomy: 'You shall worship the Lord your God, and him only shall you serve.'[15] Here, too, the temptation is more than it may seem at first sight; it offers more than the lure of temporal power. Scholars have sometimes debated whether Jesus might have felt drawn by political ambition as his ministry began. Whether he did or not, this text cannot help. Its Deuteronomic setting marks it as a temptation to prefer wealth, property, and other external possessions to God himself. Such a preference to the Father held no attractions for Jesus. He loved him with all his might.

These temptations, then, in Matthew's Gospel are more than enticements to satisfy hunger, acquire spiritual power, and gain political leadership. At one level, they reprise the drama of the Chosen People in the wilderness: the temptations to which they surrendered, Jesus resisted; at another, they represent an assault on Jesus' love for his Father to see whether he loved him indeed with all his heart and soul and might, that is, from the very roots of his being, with his entire life, and with everything he possessed. They challenge his total love. In doing so, they challenge his very identity, for what kind of Saviour would he have been, had he resorted to using his power like magic to satisfy his hunger, or had he tested his Father by leaping from the Temple, or had he worshipped the devil to gain cheap control. He is shown to be completely faithful, the steadfast son of Israel and the perfect son of the Father.

The Lucan account takes up the same material, but with

different emphases. Luke's Gospel looks consistently towards Jerusalem from the moment we learn that Jesus set his face to go there[16] and so it is natural for him to change around the second and third temptations. The final, climactic temptation in his text will take place in Jerusalem, on the pinnacle of the Temple. There are less obvious differences as well, in particular a shift away from representing the temptations of Jesus as a re-enactment of Israel's drama in the wilderness to a simpler perception of Jesus as filled by the Holy Spirit. Matthew had declared that Jesus 'was led by the Spirit into the wilderness to be tempted by the devil',[17] but there is no suggestion of any such direct purpose in Luke. He states merely that Jesus, 'full of the Holy Spirit, . . . was led by the Spirit for forty days in the wilderness, tempted by the devil.'[18]

This fullness of the Spirit in Jesus indicates his perfect trust in God. In this context, the appeal to the teaching of Deuteronomy suggests, not so much the perfection of love, as of that unreserved trust. The temptation to make bread from a stone is answered by confidence in God's word, the promise that will not fail; the temptation to temporal power is countered by the proclamation of God's sovereignty: 'him only shall you serve'; and the temptation to spiritual control is dismissed by acclaiming the graciousness of God who shall not be tempted.[19]

These accounts of the tempting of Jesus combine to teach us a powerful lesson, for they begin to show us who he was. Their different emphases are at one in presenting his solitude in the wilderness as a time which disclosed his identity. He is the one who is perfectly faithful, unfaltering in his longing for his Father and his desire to fulfil the Father's will. He could not be deflected from that purpose. In him love and trust were supreme. But Luke closes his account with a sinister sentence: 'And when the devil had ended every temptation, he departed from him until an opportune time.'[20] That time was to come in his agony and passion. The issues raised in these temptations would then be raised once more. In the meantime, however, the Gospel tells us that Jesus was transfigured.

Jesus is transfigured

Moses was not the only great figure in the Old Testament who fasted for forty days and forty nights. In the first Book of the Kings, the prophet Elijah retreated to the wilderness to escape the anger of King Ahab. He ate and drank, but then, we are told, 'went in the strength of that food forty days and forty nights to Horeb the mount of God.'[21] And there he encountered God, not in wind or fire or earthquake, but in the still small voice. Moses and Elijah are monumental figures. In their persons they symbolize the word of God, given to the people in the Law and in prophecy.

It is good to keep that in mind when we recall the occasion Jesus took with him Peter and James and John and went up the mountain.[22] Matthew and Mark speak simply of Jesus taking them apart, but Luke is explicit about their purpose. They 'went up on the mountain to pray.' Nor does Luke, unlike the others, use the word 'transfigured', but he remarks simply that, as Jesus 'was praying, the appearance of his face changed, and his clothes became dazzling white.' It seems that what is being described is not an incident plainly visible to anyone who might be passing, but rather what the disciples perceived. While Jesus was praying, they had a vision in which they saw Moses, the great lawgiver, and Elijah, the great prophet, talking to him. Luke is the only one to report the subject of their conversation: they were speaking of his 'departure, which he was about to accomplish at Jerusalem.' While Jesus was rapt in prayer, these three friends of his are presented as glimpsing his glory, his inner life. Moreover, the subject of Moses' and Elijah's conversation with Jesus, described in English as his 'departure', can be appreciated more easily when we realize that the Greek original says they were speaking of his '*exodus*'. Jesus, who in his solitude at his temptation, was seen as the faithful representative of the Chosen People, is here in this second great scene where he is at prayer, perceived by his disciples as preparing for his *exodus*, his passage to new life. And they hear a voice from the cloud which declares, 'This is my Son, my Chosen.'[23]

Temptation and transfiguration may be regarded as two sides of the same reality. What the temptations had sought to destroy, the transfiguration reveals. Jesus was tempted not to be the faithful Son of the Father; he was tempted to withdraw his perfect love and trust; he rejected these suggestions altogether. And the transfiguration disclosed his glory. On the mountain, his disciples received an awe-inspiring vision of his identity as the beloved Son, the Chosen; they glimpsed the radiance of his perfect love. Once again, in his praying Jesus' intimacy with his Father is revealed, while the reference to his exodus acts as a reminder of his fidelity to his mission.

While Luke alone speaks of this exodus, only Matthew and Mark include a conversation between the bewildered disciples and Jesus as they return down the mountain. They ask him about Elijah and why it was said that Elijah must come first. Jesus answers that Elijah comes to restore all things, that he has come but was unrecognized, and they 'did to him whatever they pleased.'[24] In Matthew the words are understood as a reference to John the Baptist. Jesus then adds that the Son of Man will also suffer at their hands. This remark, like the Lucan allusion to the exodus, points directly to his passion.

Jesus in agony

Jesus' prayer in the Garden of Gethsemane as his arrest draws near contains starkly those qualities which marked his prayer in the earlier scenes. Yet again he has taken Peter, James, and John apart from the others, but he moves away still further himself. Overcome by distress, he asks that the hour might pass from him: 'Abba, Father, for you all things are possible; remove this cup from me'; but then he adds, 'yet not what I want, but what you want.'[25] The supreme crisis makes abundantly clear his intimacy with the Father and obedience to his will.

Moreover, the Lucan Gospel which had referred darkly to the tempter's return, introduces into its account of Jesus' passion elements which take up again those first temptations. The temptation to turn a stone into bread to satisfy hunger has become a mocking challenge from the rulers and the soldiers and a desperate one from a thief crucified with him. They call to him that, if he is the Christ, he should save himself; they are inviting him to resort to magic.[26] The lure to political power had come earlier when, at the Last Supper, the disciples had been arguing about which of them was to be the greatest and were instructed to 'let the greatest among you become as the youngest, and the leader as one who serves.'[27] And the duel with the devil was resumed most explicitly at the moment of his arrest. Satan had already 'entered into Judas', who then engineered Jesus' capture.[28] 'This,' Jesus observed, 'is your hour, and the power of darkness.'[29]

(iii)

In each of these scenes Jesus is at prayer. He is not merely saying prayers; he is caught up in his longing for the Father and by his deep-rooted desire to do the Father's will. His way of praying teaches us about prayerfulness. We will need courage to learn its lesson, for when we contemplate him at prayer, we begin to see who he is. It shows us his capacity for love, an unreserved love which is prepared to accept the consequences of this loving, whatever they may be. As such, it points to his crucifixion. It is on the cross that the prayer of Jesus finds its purest expression and reveals his identity to us most clearly. In a remark of Herbert McCabe's, 'the deepest reality of Jesus is simply to be *of* the Father'.[30] We will need courage to be like him. To share this life means we must be ready to accept the demands this kind of loving will place on us.

There are threads here which we must begin to weave together. Our thoughts about Jesus at prayer, possessed by love, have brought us to his cross and so we have glimpsed our own need for courage, if we are to live as his disciples. We need to grasp more firmly the connection between his love and his barbaric crucifixion.

4

Jesus and Love

(i)

THERE is a saying which is common among Christians: 'Jesus saved us from our sins by dying on the cross.' We believe that is true. But it is also a saying which needs to be interpreted with care, because it is very concentrated; it is saying a lot in a little, and it can give rise to misunderstandings.

Adopted narrowly, it could encourage a view which emphasized the cross as the exclusive means to our salvation: it is only the cross that has saved us. By concentrating on the cross alone, we might find ourselves failing to recognize the part other aspects of Jesus' life contributed. We could neglect the implications of his birth, underestimate what we might learn from his public ministry, and relegate the significance of his resurrection and glorification to a happy postscript. And then again, we may become completely bewildered. As we are brought to reflect more and more on the death of Jesus as the only source of our salvation, we may find that we are faced with a severe difficulty. Reflection forces us to look for a reason: why should our salvation depend upon this cruel death? Why should barbarism be the price of reconciliation? We may remember old lessons about the infinite magnitude of sin as it is an offence against the infinitely good God, but we wonder why God, if he is so good, should require such a sacrifice. For justice's sake? But where is the justice when the victim is uniquely innocent? It can make our heads spin. Can God be good? Does God exist?

We believe indeed that Jesus saved us from our sins by dying on the cross, but we must also acknowledge that this saying is highly compressed. If we are to understand it correctly, we must begin again from a fresh vantage point. We must begin from love.

(ii)

We believe that God created us out of love. We must not presume to know too much about God, but if we are right about anything we affirm of him, we can say that love is of his very essence. Love is not God; we do not deify the quality; but God is love. Whatever explanations there may be for our existence, we believe that the most profound cause for our being is God's love for us. He has loved us into life. And his love is without reserve. There is no limit to his love for us. There is no evil so vile that it could bring his love to an end. We may not love God; we may live lives inspired by cold, calculating malice; we may retreat from him, overwhelmed with loathing, to the furthest reaches of hell; but we cannot prevent God from loving us, for we cannot stop God from being God. God is love.

At the same time, we know that love is not dictatorial. It does not coerce. And so we can resist it. We believe in fact that from the beginning of human life, we have resisted it, not all the time, not in everything we have done, but consistently that thread has run through human affairs, the instinct which resists love. We call that instinct original sin; it is the origin, the source, of our sinning. The resistance itself is sin.

It is possible to compound the fault. Left to our own devices, our resistance to love is reinforced. We can raise the barricades and make our loveless condition secure. But God is love. He will never impose, but he will implore. And he will act. We believe that God so loved the world that at the appointed time he sent his only Son: the Word of God became flesh; Jesus, who is the Christ, was born. He came to reveal the Father's love, to break down the barricades, to overcome human resistance to love. That was the heart of his mission: to reveal divine love; to recall us men and women to its ways, so as to overcome

our resistance, heal our sins, and reconcile us to the Father. We
are becoming familiar with this teaching.

In the Marcan Gospel Jesus opens his ministry by announcing:
'The time is fulfilled, and the kingdom of God has come near;
repent and believe in the good news.'[1] This proclamation of the
kingdom would have been understood as the time when God's
power and judgement would be displayed and his rule over
creation established. It called for a change of heart, for repentance. But Jesus was always anxious to explain that this power
and rule, this kingdom, was not to be conceived in familiar
political terms. St Mark's Gospel is characterized by that theme
which scholars have called the messianic secret. It is their way
of accounting for a curious feature in the Gospel: while Jesus
has come to make himself known as the Christ and leads his
disciples to this understanding of his identity, he also insists that
they tell no one about it. At the very central moment of the
Gospel, he asks them, 'Who do people say that I am?' They
offer him various answers. He then asks them for their opinion
and Peter answers, 'You are the Messiah.' And at once we are
told, 'he sternly ordered them not to tell anyone about him.'[2]
The most probable reason for this alliance of disclosure and
secrecy is the popular expectation that the Messiah would be a
political figure. That was not how Jesus saw himself. His teaching
was based on the commandment of love.

According to the Gospels of Matthew and Luke, a lawyer asks
Jesus a question as a test, but in Mark's Gospel a scribe approaches
him. We are told that he has been listening to a dispute between
Jesus and various Pharisees, Herodians, and Sadducees. One area
of dispute, incidentally – in Matthew as well, but not in Luke,
where it is introduced later – was the political issue of the
propriety of paying taxes to Caesar. Be that as it may, this
scribe has been listening and has been impressed. His question
is respectful. He asks, 'Which commandment is the first of all?'
It was a favourite question to put to a teacher; people wanted
to know their priorities. And Jesus answered him by quoting the
Shema Israel: ' "Hear, O Israel: the Lord our God, the Lord is

one: and you shall love the Lord your God with all your heart, and with all your soul, and with all your mind, and with all your strength." The second is this, "You shall love your neighbour as yourself." There is no other commandment greater than these.'[3] Here is the heart of the gospel. You will remember that the temptations which Jesus underwent in the wilderness formed in part an assault on this fundamental teaching.

All the same, this teaching would have made no impression had it been a matter of words and no more. But the Gospel picture of Jesus shows us a man whose actions confirm his words. He was driven by love. He loved his heavenly Father and he cared for the blind, the deaf and the dumb, the lame and the paralysed, the possessed and the poor. He mixed with tax collectors and prostitutes. He was not afraid to be the friend of those whom society despised. Professor Geza Vermes has noted how Jesus differed from his contemporaries and even his prophetic predecessors in one way more than any other:

> The prophets spoke on behalf of the honest poor, and defended the widows and the fatherless, those oppressed and exploited by the wicked, rich and powerful. Jesus went further. In addition to proclaiming these blessed, he actually took his stand among the pariahs of his world, those despised by the respectable. Sinners were his table companions and the ostracised tax-collectors and prostitutes his friends.[4]

When he found people in need, he did not spare himself. Early in St Mark's Gospel, as we noticed earlier,[5] a day is described when Jesus went to Capernaum on the Sabbath, taught there and cured a man with an unclean spirit, went on to Simon's house where he cured Simon's mother-in-law, and later that evening attended to the sick who were brought to him. The pace of the narrative suggests an exhausting day.[6] Again, some time later, when the disciples have come back to Jesus after their first experience of their ministry – a combination of word and action, preaching repentance, casting out demons, and anointing and healing the sick – he takes them away to rest in a lonely place. He is showing them consideration. However, his plan is thwarted as the people guess where he is going and arrive before him. When he sees them, we are told, he has 'compassion on them, because they were like sheep without a shepherd; and he began to teach them many things.'[7] Once again the image presented is clear: here is one who cares for those in need.

The reaction to such generosity seems predictable in theory, but in practice it can be very different. We might presume that such kindness would inspire acceptance: here after all was good news. Everyone wants to be loved. What better news could there be in the midst of human struggles than a revelation of God's abiding love for us by proclaiming the defeat of evil and making it manifest by healing the sick, caring for the despised, and forgiving sins? Yet Jesus was rejected.

A number of factors conspired to bring his mission to its ruinous end. Vermes's assessment offers clues. The religious authorities were hostile to the reforms that Jesus' teaching implied; the Romans were suspicious of the unrest the Galilean might cause; and then there was Judas. Was Judas greedy or did he hope rather to galvanize his friend into action by creating a crisis? We shall never know. The Gospels indicate that Jesus was aware of the disaster awaiting him; he predicted it;[8] but he never faltered. He knew he had to fulfil his Father's will and make known the good news of his love, whatever the consequences might be. The consequences played an indispensable role. Their acceptance revealed this unfailing love.

We have acknowledged already the teaching that the Father loves us without limit and the Son came to reveal that love. But what does it mean to say, 'without limit'? That is a measurement and how is love to be measured? Is it ever possible to judge that one person is loved more than another? Perhaps it is.

Sacrifice or self-denial can measure love. How much hardship will we endure for another? It depends how much we love them. We may hurry past some unknown person who is being mugged, saying guiltily to ourselves, 'It's nothing to do with me, I haven't time, I must get on.' But should we return home to find our mother or father, brother or sister, husband or wife, son or daughter, being attacked, we rush to the rescue. The risk may be far greater than at the scene in the street, but we act without hesitation, because we love more. King Solomon had no difficulty in determining which of the two women before him was the true mother of the child each claimed as her own; it was, of course, the one who was ready to sacrifice her claim, and so would have lost the child for herself, in order to save his life.[9] Some years ago, the son of friends of mine was killed in a car accident. His father told me that one day at mass he had suddenly thought that there was nothing special about Jesus dying on the cross; if you love enough, to give up your life is easy; he would willingly have given up his own in order for his son to be alive again.

Jesus is the faithful one. His entire life was shaped by an interior disposition of perfect love and obedience. He loved his Father and was obedient to the Father's will; he loved all men and women and was obedient to their needs. It was the Father's will that he minister to those needs. That was his mission. There was a perfect correspondence in his obedience. Inspired by love, he is the faithful one. He accepted the consequences of his loving even to suffering death on a cross: 'Greater love has no man than this, that a man lay down his life for his friends.'[10] Whom has Jesus not befriended?

So the cross on which Jesus died comes gradually into perspective. Jesus came to save us from our sins, not, first of all, by dying on the cross, but by revealing to us the overwhelming love the Father has for us. It was his fidelity to that mission whatever the outcome, which led to his cruel death. But to say this is not to diminish the cross. The horror of what he had to undergo cannot be exaggerated. Such a death makes plain the depth and quality of his love.

(iii)

Jesus suffered physically. That is most obvious. He was beaten casually and formally scourged. Thorns were pressed into his skull like a mock crown. He carried for a while the beam of the cross on which he was to die. And he was crucified. Nails were hammered through his wrists; his legs were bent beneath him and further nails driven through his ankles; and so he was fastened there. The weight of his body would have sent crippling pain along his arms and forced the air from his lungs. To relieve this suffocation the crucified would have raised himself, levering himself up by stretching his bent knees and so allowing the air to fill his lungs again. Then the pain and the weight of his body would have forced him gradually to sink down once more. Crucifixion is a cruel form of execution, not simply because of the suffering it inflicts, but also because it is slow. The condemned man can hardly prevent himself from prolonging his agony as his sufferings cause him to shift and writhe; he tries instinctively to ease their excruciating intensity. At last, exhausted, he can move no more, can gather no more air into his lungs, and suffocates. There can be no doubt that Jesus suffered physically.

He suffered personally as well. Judas, his friend, betrayed him. The motive is irrelevant. Judas, we are told, kept the common purse. People do not usually put money at risk. It is reasonable to suppose that among the Twelve Judas stood out for his reliability; but he was the one who handed Jesus over. Peter, to whom he had promised so much and who had protested his loyalty so vigorously, then disowned him. The rest fled. They left Jesus to be mocked, an object of scorn amongst those who had welcomed him enthusiastically into Jerusalem a few days earlier. The Fourth Gospel tells us that the beloved disciple remained close by with some women from their company and that Mary, the mother of Jesus, was among them. Seeing her grief can only have added to his sorrow. Jesus suffered personally, and it may be that that was not the limit of his suffering.

Is it not possible that Jesus in his passion underwent a desolating spiritual agony as well? I am not thinking simply of the cry from the cross, 'My God, my God, why have you forsaken me?' which is found in the Marcan and Matthaean tradition of the passion.[11] It may be significant, but can also be interpreted as a reminder of Psalm 22 and a cry of triumph. I do not want to depend on it. I am thinking rather of the fact that Jesus had not come to Jerusalem to die, but to make known the good news of the Father's healing love. Though he expected the worst, as those Gospel prophecies of his passion indicate, he must have been encouraged by the welcoming crowds who came out to cheer him when he entered the city the day after the Sabbath. Before the next Sabbath began, his body had been removed from the cross. Hopes had been dashed. His ministry was in ruins. We do not know how he felt during those final hours of torture, humiliation, and execution, but it is possible that he underwent something like that 'death of self' which spiritual writers have described. No single individual can suffer all particular sufferings, but a person may suffer every kind of suffering, physical, personal, and mental or spiritual. We know that Jesus endured the first two. May he not have undergone the third? What would that have been like for him? Let me make use of Jock Dalrymple once again.

Towards the end of his book, *Costing Not Less Than Everything*, Dalrymple describes in simple terms this condition of spiritual desolation. It is extreme and not everyone plumbs its depths; those who do will not necessarily be afflicted with all its symptoms: we need not suppose, for example, that Jesus felt a 'nameless mood of despair and self-hate'; but his self-confidence may have evaporated like the mist; he may have questioned his own worth, felt no good, hollow, a sham, a cause of harm to those who dealt with him; he may have felt desperately alone, frightened, unaccepted, as he certainly was rejected. A kind of fog may have permeated every corner of his mind. There is nothing we believe about Jesus which need make him immune from this kind of desolating spiritual agony.[12] On the contrary, it seems unlikely that the Master would have shielded himself from a kind of suffering to which so many of his disciples would be vulnerable. All the same, it raises a question which will occur readily to a number of people.

If Jesus was so overwhelmed in his passion, they will ask, what hope have we? And indeed, they will argue, he could not have been so afflicted because, although truly human, he was also truly God and, because God, possessed divine knowledge. He knew all the time, therefore, the reason for his sufferings, their brevity, and their joyous outcome in resurrection. In other words, throughout his appalling sufferings, Jesus understood fully that what was happening to him was part of the Father's plan for our salvation. He was not bewildered by what was done to him; he had no sense of failure, in fact, could have none. Although a man, because he was also God, divine knowledge enlightened every step of his final ordeal.

We need to proceed carefully. We believe that Jesus was God and so enjoyed divine consciousness and knowledge. But none of us knows what it would be like to possess such consciousness and knowledge. On the other hand, we can, I think, say what it would not be like: it is not simply a matter of possessing solutions to all the human problems which remain unsolved by human means alone. Divine knowledge is a different *kind* of knowledge, not just a supplement to human knowledge. It is not as though the human Jesus was aware of all our questions, while the divine Christ supplied the answers and so shielded him from the anxieties which lack of knowledge creates. Yet when people appeal to Jesus' divine knowledge and consciousness in a way that would protect him from the spiritual sufferings of his passion, that is what they are saying. Let me offer a light-hearted illustration. I am reminded of a day when I was ten. The maths teacher left his textbook in the classroom by accident, and we pupils were delighted. This textbook, of course, was exactly like ours, except in one particular: as well as the questions, it included a supplement with all the answers. When people invoke Jesus' divine knowledge as the reason for his immunity from any sense of bewilderment, darkness, and failure in his passion, it is not divine knowledge they invoke, but a kind of superhuman knowledge, like that supplement with the answers to the unanswered questions. Whatever divine knowledge may have meant for Jesus, it cannot have meant that. Such knowledge could only compromise the genuineness of his human experience. Instead we are able to glimpse at least a little the way the splendour of divine knowledge and the limitations of human knowledge are compatible. And we should be grateful.[13]

Jesus was like us in all things except sin. He was as much a prey to confusion and distress, a sense of failure and defeat, as any one of us. That is why we can trust him and follow him. He has gone before us. He knows the way. He has known the bitter depths in which we can feel ourselves lost. And we follow him as both the divine Son and our human brother. As the Father's Son he was sent to reveal God's love for us and as our brother he experiences genuinely our condition. The wonder of the mystery is the way the divine and human are perfectly at one in him, while they maintain their distinct integrity. We follow Jesus, who is divine, but not because his divinity was cushioning him from the consequences of his unlimited love in his passion, but because, no matter how desperate his circumstances became – whether physical, personal, or spiritual – he remained utterly steadfast in his love for the Father and for us and in his commitment to fulfilling the Father's will. He did not lead the human blind out of their darkness by taking advantage of divine sight, but by his fidelity in love. That is why, in spite of the sufferings which overwhelmed him, he gives us hope. He calls us to the same fidelity.

On the face of it there could be no more welcome invitation. But delight in the call is soon tempered by experience. Our world is not hospitable to love. When St Paul wrote, 'Love is patient; love is kind; love is not jealous or boastful; it is not arrogant or rude. Love does not insist on its own way; it is not irritable or resentful; it does not rejoice at wrong, but rejoices in the right', he was not describing a way of living that

self-evidently holds sway in human society.[14] Jesus knew that and
warned those who liked to listen to him that, if they were to
accept his invitation and follow his way, they too would have
to take up the cross.[15] The pattern cannot be avoided. And the
cross comes in many forms. It is easily found.

(iv)

Our world is dark. We turn to love in the hope of lightening it,
but find instead a gap that appals us between the love that is
proclaimed and the evil – sometimes moral, sometimes natural –
that afflicts our condition. It is that evil which seems to make a
mockery of love. It brings it into disrepute.

We see natural disasters, earthquake, famine, and flood, and
the death from disease of countless innocent children. Where
is the love of the loving Creator God to be found in all that?
Next, there are the injustices which scar our world, war and
conflict, genocide and ethnic-cleansing, corruption and criminal
violence, abject poverty and homelessness. Where can the
victims of these terrors find love? Then there is the vast range of
human misery and tragedy: broken, failed, and loveless marriages;
neglectful parents and estranged or abused children; betrayal
by friends; unemployment, redundancy, and loss of self-esteem;
sickness and handicap; alcoholism and drug addiction; the suicide
of those we love; terminal illness and bereavement; the list can
go on and on. We find ourselves gazing out over a bleak land-
scape. We may realize that sometimes we have helped to cause
these situations by our own wrongdoing; we are not disclaiming
all responsibility; but we know at other times we have truly been
acting for the best and yet our efforts have come to nothing and
the situation has spun out of control. In any event, circumstances
have developed which leave us powerless, at their mercy. The
appeal to love may seem like a cruel joke. It is more likely to
provoke anger.

What can we do? How can a loving God allow such things
to happen? Let us take the questions in reverse order.

It is natural to ask why God, if he is so good and infinitely loving, should allow these terrible evils to assault us. We call him almighty, all-powerful. Why does he not prevent them? He could stop them, we say. Why doesn't he? We would, if we could. As it is, there are good people who offer their skills, provide money, and pour out their energy in an attempt to prevent and overcome the horrors that bear down on us. They occur nevertheless because, when everything possible has been done, it is still not enough. If we had the power, we would not allow such things to happen. But God, who, it is alleged, has the power, seems indifferent. He does nothing. Who can believe in such a God? The force of the argument seems unassailable. Is there anything further to be said? I believe there is.

It may help to recognize that the argument is based on an understanding of divine power which goes hand-in-glove with the view of divine knowledge we considered earlier. There we discovered that what was called divine knowledge was in fact a kind of superhuman knowledge; here what is called divine power is shown on examination to be only a kind of superhuman power, a supplement to human capability. As before, I can make no claim to know what divine power is, but I am confident that it is not to be conceived simply as an excess of human power. Just as divine knowledge is a kind of knowledge distinct from human knowledge, so divine power is a kind of power distinct from human power. The argument that revolves around an appeal to God to intervene and rescue us from the evil consequences of our condition by exercising his power, although common, is based on a misconception of the nature of that divine power. We need to appeal not to his power, but to his love.

We believe that God loves this world which he has created. Why did he include natural disasters within his creation, earthquake, famine, disease, and drought? Why is there evil at all? Why did our loving, all-powerful God not create a universe and a human society within it which were harmonious and perfectly good? We cannot presume to answer such ancient questions definitively, but perhaps our growing awareness of our environment gives us a clue.

We now realize more than any earlier generation that we cannot be distinguished from our world, our environment. To use the image, we are not like actors on a set. At Universal Studios they show you how ET could fly on his bicycle, sitting motionless in the studio against a filmed backdrop. Our lives are not like that. We are on location. We cannot be distinguished from our world. We are a part of it. Change the environment so that such disasters never occur and you change everything, including us. In a different environment, we would be different as well. The human race has developed as it has because it lives in this environment, but this environment, this atmosphere, these weather patterns, give us flood and famine, earthquake and disease. We are who we are. And God does not abandon us.

That truth is illustrated classically by Elie Wiesel in his memoir, *Night*, his account of his experience and survival as a Jewish teenager during the Second World War. He tells there of his time in Buna when three people were hanged. One of them was a young boy. The electric power station had been blown up and he was implicated. He was questioned, tortured, and sentenced to death. The inmates of the camp had to march past the victims. The two adults cried out, 'Long live liberty', but the child was silent. And Wiesel heard someone behind him ask, 'Where is God? Where is He?'

> At a sign from the head of the camp, the three chairs tipped over. Total silence throughout the camp. On the horizon, the sun was setting.
>
> 'Bare your heads!' yelled the head of the camp. His voice was raucous. We were weeping.
>
> 'Cover your heads!'
>
> Then the march past began. The two adults were no longer alive. Their tongues hung swollen, blue-tinged. But the third rope was still moving; being so light, the child was still alive . . .

For more than half an hour he stayed there, struggling
between life and death, dying in slow agony under our
eyes. And we had to look him full in the face. He was still
alive when I passed in front of him. His tongue was still red,
his eyes were not yet glazed.

Behind me, I heard the same man asking: 'Where is God
now?'

And I heard a voice within me answer him: 'Where is
He? Here He is – He is hanging here on this gallows . . .'

That night the soup tasted of corpses.[16]

God does not abandon us.

And so the second question: what are we to do?

The antidote to these disasters – and the moral evils which
also afflict us and for which we have some responsibility – is not
to be found by invoking a 'divine', but actually superhuman,
power, but by living according to the love that Jesus revealed.
That is not a soft lesson; it is perhaps the hardest of all for it
means entering the heart of darkness.

We have seen that the faithful love Jesus revealed is a love
without limit. It brought him to the cross. His execution was
not a sly manoeuvre, a clever, subtle strategy by which he gained
success and triumph. In itself it was unrelieved defeat. It is a
frightening truth to accept. We Christians have spent much time
over the past two thousand years trying to avoid the lesson of
that crucifixion by explaining its horror away. We have wanted
Jesus to have it all planned, to have known what was taking
place, to be in control. It was not like that. We should thank
God it was not like that, for from the darkest depths of that
defeat we are redeemed. There is no darkness in which he has
not shared and which he has not overcome. He has triumphed,
but not because the darkness was illusory, the horror a charade,
the defeat unreal. Jesus has triumphed because, even when he
was most desolate, he remained perfectly faithful in love.

We are called to follow him. In doing so, we must accept our
crosses in whatever form they may take. We have to enter the

darkness and face it. Think of Francesca Luard, beautiful and
gifted and rare, not promiscuous nor a drug addict, but she died
from AIDS-related cancer in November 1994. When telling her
story, she wrote: 'The only time I get religious is when I'm very
unhappy. I place myself in God's hands as if I were a baby, and
I feel safe.'[17] These words are not escapism, cheap comfort. Her
courage was extraordinary. They illustrate rather the way in
which in moments of crisis we take stock. Think also of Cardinal
Basil Hume who remarked that 'the real cross is the one you
have not chosen, the one that does not fit neatly on your
shoulder'; it is rough, wounding, and life-draining; and then he
added the advice offered by a Mother Superior to a grumbling
nun, 'Don't drag your cross, carry it'.[18] In the midst of derel-
iction, we must keep our hearts open and generous and filled
with love, as Jesus did, and then we will find ourselves being led
out of the darkness of unconditional defeat to new life.

5

Risen in Glory to New Life

WE say that Jesus was raised to new life. He moved from the darkness of the cross to the glory of the resurrection. By our baptism, we believe that we already share in some way in that new life. But in what way? How has his resurrection already become ours? We need to try to understand the resurrection better in order to see more clearly its significance for us. It takes me back to Easter 1988.

That Holy Saturday I was stuck. Major feasts offer a particular challenge to the preacher. What can be said within ten minutes which a congregation has not heard before? It is not a question of straining after novelty: the old message must be proclaimed. But we have to look for fresh ways of drawing people more deeply into the mystery. By mid-afternoon I still had no idea how I might preach on the resurrection at the Vigil that evening. The longer I sat at my desk the blanker my mind became. So I went outside for a breath of air. I was working at the Oxford University Chaplaincy at the time and, as I strolled along Rose Place beside the building, I bent down absent-mindedly to pick up a piece of paper which was littering the path. It was a page torn from an old *Reader's Digest* and it contained a number of quotations. One was a saying of Chief Crowfoot of the Blackfoot Indians on his deathbed in Alberta. He had declared that life is 'as the flash of the firefly in the night. It is as the breath of the buffalo in the wintertime. It is as the little shadow that runs across the grass and loses itself in the sunset'. Chief Crowfoot, I have learned, was a wise man, greatly admired. As a description of this life's brevity, his words are touched with beauty, but can they stand as a statement about life itself? They do not express what Christians believe. I had found the prompt I needed for my homily.

In our search for life's meaning, the flash of the firefly, the breath of the buffalo, and the shadow on the grass will not do. We turn instead to the resurrection of Jesus.

We believe not only that Jesus died, but that he was raised from the dead. However, when we speak of his resurrection, we are not simply affirming his continuing influence as an impressive individual, as though on reflection the followers of Jesus decided to go on living in accordance with the values he had championed. Nor are we talking about resuscitation. There are accounts in the Gospels of Jesus restoring people to life – Jairus's daughter, the son of the widow of Nain, and Lazarus.[1] They would all die again, because they had returned from death to this life. That is not what we believe about Jesus. When he rose from the dead, he had passed from this life through death to a new life beyond this one. He would not die again. His resurrection reveals an essential truth about the meaning of our lives, their shape and pattern. It is not a truth easily grasped.

The Gospels try to capture the extraordinary character of the resurrection by including in their accounts of Jesus risen from the dead two elements, one mysterious, the other immediate. So the disciples on the road to Emmaus do not at first recognize Jesus, but they have a meal with him;[2] nor is he recognized by Mary Magdalene when she visits the tomb, but then she can cling to his feet;[3] and we are told that Jesus enters the upper room where the disciples are gathered, although the door is locked, and then he shows them his hands and his side.[4] Both elements are important. The mysterious – the failure to recognize him, the appearance in a locked room – is teaching us a lesson about the new life which Jesus has entered: he is not as he was before; while the immediate – the sharing of a meal, the reference to the physical – saves us from supposing that the disciples' experience was an illusion: they were not hallucinating, victims of group hysteria. He was really there, present with them, but in a way quite unlike anything they had known previously.

This combination of the mysterious and the immediate invites us to contemplate more deeply the mystery of Jesus' resurrection. The relationship between what is familiar, on the one hand, and what is utterly new and different, on the other, is very difficult to grasp. We are saying that the risen Jesus was at the same time utterly different from what the disciples had known before, and yet recognizable and familiar. They were able to say, 'It is the Lord.'[5] As the *Catechism* declares: '[The] risen body in which he appears to them is the same body that had been tortured and crucified, for it still bears the traces of his Passion. Yet at the same time this authentic, real body possesses the new properties of a glorious body'.[6] James Alison in his book, *Knowing Jesus*, has helped to shed valuable light on this profound question.

He remarks that meeting the risen Jesus

> was not a case of encountering something familiar in the midst of what is other. It was not as if, lost in Tibet, you suddenly come across someone who offered you tea and biscuits like in England. That would be to suggest that Jesus had somehow 'passed over', and was a bit of who he had been now stuck in another world.

He would have returned, but would not have changed significantly; he would have been completely familiar, instantly recognizable; as Alison observes, 'we would be in the realm of ghosts, and spirit divination'. And he goes on:

> No, what the disciples were able to experience was that the wholly, gratuitously other, was made present as a giving back of someone familiar.

In other words, the risen Jesus was not recognized because he was unchanged; on the contrary, he was changed utterly; and the wonder lies in the fact that, in spite of so total a change, he was recognized by the disciples as familiar, as 'a presence of recognizable, familiar love for them'.[7]

It was not a matter of someone returning from the dead and being recognized; that would have been like seeing a ghost; rather it was a question of someone who has passed through death to a new kind of life, one utterly beyond our experience or power of imagining, who is none the less known as familiar. The risen Jesus is transformed beyond all recognition. Yet the one who appeared to the disciples was also familiar.

A further particularly powerful element in this understanding is the *way* it holds together the utterly other and the familiar. We tend to think chronologically: Jesus was crucified and then he was raised. And, of course, that was how the disciples experienced the events. But it is wise to see that it was not like that for Jesus. To borrow a neat illustration from James Alison, we can suppose that Jesus' birthday fell on Holy Saturday. And so, 'He was thirty-three when he was killed on Good Friday. But he was not thirty-four when he rose on Easter Sunday. He was not any age at all. He was his whole human life and death given back to God.'[8] The one who was raised has not been cured of being slaughtered: the risen Lord *is* the crucified Jesus.[9]

To say that, however, could cause alarm. Does it mean that, although risen, the passion of Jesus is continuing? The point is important for us. We believe that we have been brought to share in Christ's death by our baptism so that we might walk with him, as St Paul says, in newness of life.[10] Does it mean that, when we rise again in Christ, we are still carrying our crosses? We had hoped to leave them behind. We need to be clear.

When someone we love dies, we mourn them. Their loss is like a wound. When we emerge from grief, it is not as though we no longer mind their being dead. We carry the wound still, perhaps even more deeply; but we are reconciled to the new situation. The crucifying and raising of Jesus are a little like that. The resurrection does not annihilate the crucifixion, make it as though it had never happened. When we say the risen Lord is the crucified Jesus, we are trying to express the deep truth that in his resurrection the whole of who Jesus is is taken up and brought to its fulfilment. Resurrection takes hold even of death and transforms it. It does not cancel the past, but it heals it.

This truth is profoundly significant for us, because by our baptism we are invited and called already in this life to share in the death and resurrection of Jesus. It is not an invitation simply for the life to come. And in this life, as we know all too well, there is more than one crisis or trial, more than one cross to carry. The dying and the rising are woven into the very fabric of our daily lives. The resurrection is teaching us that, when we are grafted on to Christ through our baptism, the meaning of our lives is transformed. The whole of our existence takes on a new meaning. How?

(ii)

Consider the disciples. What had happened to them?

When Jesus had been arrested, they were overcome with fear and scattered. Then they came together again for safety behind locked doors in the upper room. The Gospels show us men demoralized, their dream in ruins. But seven weeks later, when Pentecost came round, they had changed. They went out into the streets of Jerusalem to proclaim to everyone they met that the Jesus who had been crucified just before Passover and who had died, had been raised from the dead. They were themselves, they said, witnesses to his resurrection. Persecution and imprisonment, flogging and execution could not make them change their story. They had been transformed. But what had happened in fact? What had they witnessed?

One fascinating feature of our Liturgy for Holy Saturday night is that the Gospels for all three years contain no significant account of an appearance of Jesus risen from the dead. Matthew and Mark speak of a young man in a white robe who announces to Mary Magdalene and the women with her that Jesus has risen, and in Luke there are two men in brilliant clothes who deliver the message.[11] A slight exception can be found in Matthew's account. As the women run from the tomb to give the news, they meet Jesus, but little that is significant is added. He merely repeats the message they had already received. In other words, it is a night about faith, not about sight. Mary delivers the news, which Luke tells us was not believed. But, according to Luke, it prompts Peter to visit Jesus' tomb and he comes away 'wondering at what had happened'.[12] In the Fourth Gospel, both Peter and the beloved disciple go to the tomb, and the disciple, we are told, when he entered the tomb, saw and believed.[13] What happened to the disciples was a matter of faith. They received it as a gift. They did not believe, because they saw, but they saw, because they believed.

I am not suggesting that the resurrection can be explained as the consequence of their credulity. Jesus was truly risen. But he was seen because they believed. Their faith may have been a poor, inarticulate thing – the later Marcan ending has Jesus rebuking them for its weakness[14] – but it lay at the root of their experience. And it lies at the root of ours. We believe because they believed. Our response is like theirs. Faith is born from faith.

An obvious objection to this view, of course, is the case of Thomas who said he would not believe until he had placed his finger into the marks of the nails and his hand into the wound in Jesus' side. Jesus came again, confronted him, and told him, 'Blessed are those who have not seen and yet believe.'[15] But I wonder whether we are dealing with a genuine absence of all faith in Thomas. Did he see the risen Jesus without really believing at all? I do not think so.

There seems rather to have been a streak of passionate loyalty in Thomas. When Jesus planned to visit Martha and Mary after the death of their brother, Lazarus, the other disciples tried to dissuade him, for they feared his life would be in danger. Jesus, however, insisted. Then Thomas spoke up: 'Let us also go, that we may die with him.'[16] It may be that the seeds of what we call his doubt can be explained by that loyalty. So when his friends came and told him that they had seen Jesus alive, risen from the dead, the news for Thomas was too good to be true.

Perhaps he could not cope with such news being false. Perhaps he did not truly lack faith, but had been too wounded himself by his friend's execution not to need more reassurance than the declaration of the others. Thomas may not be the exception people so often suppose.

The disciples believed and so we believe. Faith is born from faith. But their experience was also special. They saw Jesus when he had been raised in a privileged way.

The appearance on the shore of the Sea of Galilee is particularly moving. Here, in the first place, the mysterious and the immediate are mingled most poignantly. Peter and some of the others have gone fishing and had no luck all night. At daybreak Jesus greets them from the shore, but they do not recognize him. He gives them directions which they follow and bring in a great haul of fish. Only then does the beloved disciple say, 'It is the Lord.' He recognizes him, sees what is familiar. And on the beach a charcoal fire has been prepared, fish are on it, and they are invited to eat breakfast. Here there has been the mysterious lack of recognition and the immediacy of breakfast. And shortly afterwards, these two elements are brought together. We are told that the others did not 'dare' to ask Jesus who he was, because 'they knew it was the Lord'. Why would they have needed to dare to ask if they already knew? The combination indicates the extraordinary nature of what they are witnessing.[17]

Then there follows the conversation between Jesus and Peter. Three times Jesus asks Peter, 'Simon, son of John, do you love me more than these?'[18] It is common to see these questions as allowing Peter to reverse his triple denial of Jesus during the passion. On the third occasion, the word used for 'love' implies a deeper, more personal friendship. It may be merely stylistic. Scholars debate the point. But the repeated question heightens the intensity of the exchange and we are told, 'Peter was grieved because he said to him the third time, "Do you love me?" And he said to him, "Lord, you know everything; you know that I love you." ' Besides his love and the hurt, Peter may have experienced a wide range of emotions, bewilderment, awe, delight, and fear. It was a moment of crisis, a moment of conversion, a moment when everything comes to be seen differently. And it must be so for us.

We believe that Jesus has risen in glory to new life. Through faith and by virtue of our baptism, we have been brought to a share in that new life, as Peter had been. Faith is born from faith. This new life is offered to us now. The same question is also put to us: 'Do you love me?' We can rejoice in the question. But if we answer 'yes', there are consequences.

(iii)

To live now according to the new life of Jesus is to try daily to perfect our faithful loving. It is not an easy path, free from struggles and trials. We ourselves still sin and we can still be disappointed and betrayed, fall sick and suffer; we will share the burdens of those we love and mourn them when they die. We are not protected from all of that. In this life cross and resurrection are entwined. We have seen that already. But if we are faithful in our loving, with hearts that are generous and remain open, not only will those crosses be transformed, but the very quality of our lives changes. This new life is a life for others. Jesus said, 'The Son of man came not to be served, but to serve, and to give his life a ransom for many.'[19] As disciples of the Master, we become instruments of what we have received. We share it with others.

Jesus said, 'I am the vine, you are the branches . . . My Father is glorified by this, that you bear much fruit'.[20] It is a demanding image. The grapes do not appear on the vine stem; they appear on the branches. If the vine is to bear fruit, it does so through its branches. If Jesus, who identifies himself as the vine, is to achieve his purpose, then he chooses to do so through us, the branches. We are the indispensable means. That is what the image is telling us.[21] And it requires a relationship in which life is shared, because, 'Just as the branch cannot bear fruit by itself unless it abides in the vine, neither can you,' Jesus adds, 'unless you abide in me.'[22] We are not simply meant to be morally decent, to give a good example, be generous and warm-hearted. Fine as that may be, it is external. It is not enough. We are to share life itself. We must be so faithful in love that Christ's life is communicated to others. It is a formidable undertaking. But it does happen.

Bishop John Taylor, the former Bishop of Winchester, gave a memorable example during his University Mission in Oxford in 1986. He quoted from a radio talk given by Dr Elisabeth Kubler-Ross, who has pioneered ameliorative work among the very old, in which she described a typical institution she had visited:

> They were all sitting half dead in their wheel-chairs, mostly paralysed and just existing, they didn't live. They watched some television, but if you had asked them what they had watched they probably would not have been able to tell you. We brought in a young woman who was a dancer and we told her to play beautiful, old-fashioned music. She brought in Tchaikovsky records and so on and started to dance among these old people, all in their wheel-chairs, which had been set in a circle. In no time the old people started to move. One old man stared at his hand and said, 'Oh, my God, I haven't moved this hand in ten years.' And the 104-year-old, in a thick German accent, said, 'That reminds me of when I danced for the Tsar of Russia.'[23]

There in a wonderful manner where ordinary daily life is shared, people come alive.

Other situations can be more demanding, particularly when someone has died. I have known people who, having been acutely bereaved and in mourning, were somehow shielded from a sharpness of grief which they could not perhaps have borne at that time, while a friend, close to them, but not necessarily that intimate, has suffered deeply. It is as though, in the heat of the crisis, the friend has carried the family's grief. I once asked someone with long and close experience of hospice care whether she knew of such experiences. She confirmed that that kind of transference of the burden does occur.

And I think of a story told about Archbishop Michael Ramsey. On one occasion while he was Archbishop of Canterbury, he was visiting New York for meetings. At the end of a long day and very tired, he was making his way quietly through the cathedral when a woman stopped him. She asked him to bless a crucifix. He was very weary but he took the cross in his hands and so concentrated over it in prayer that the woman was amazed. She took a step backwards and exclaimed, 'Truly, you are a child of God.' Such familiarity with God cannot be pretence. It comes from hours of prayer and from allowing the crucified and risen Lord to dwell deeply within us.

That indwelling is personal and individual for all those who live in Christ. And it is more than that. It is a reality also for the body of Christ which is the Church.

6

The Church as Communion

WHAT does it mean to be the Church? The question naturally invites different replies, depending on the context, but here we are asking it while we explore living Catholicism. Let us go back to the beginning.

Seven weeks after they had first seen Jesus risen from the dead, the apostles were all gathered together. Judas had committed suicide, but Matthias had been elected to take his place, so there were twelve of them. Then something happened. It is not described precisely. The brief account we have is made up of similes and images: there was a sound 'like the rush of a mighty wind'; tongues 'as of fire' appeared to divide and rest on them; and they began to speak in other languages. But they understood their experience: they were all filled with the Holy Spirit.[1] It was the day of Pentecost.

Think about the group that was gathered, those Twelve and possibly some other disciples including women, members of Jesus' family, and his mother, Mary, as well. There may have been others. What had happened to them that day? They already had a great deal in common. They were friends of Jesus and of one another; they believed in him; they had taken part in his ministry; they had many shared experiences; they had seen him crucified; in particular, they were witnesses to his resurrection. What they shared, however, they shared as individuals. The presence of the Spirit, who is the Spirit of Christ, changed that. They were no longer just individuals who shared a common life and many experiences. Now they were united by that Spirit and so had become the body of Christ. What they were as one body was greater than who they had been as a collection of individuals. They were the Church. At Pentecost the Church was born. Moreover, they were the Catholic Church, even before they left that place to proclaim their message in the streets of Jerusalem.

That may seem odd at first, a Catholic, universal Church, confined to a single room. We need to remember that catholicity is not principally a matter of size or quantity. As a young student in 1964 I read *Catholicism* by the French Jesuit, Henri de Lubac. Published in 1946 it is a serene piece of writing. One passage immediately made a deep impression on me. De Lubac qualifies the notion that the Church is Catholic because it is the largest Christian body and to be found everywhere. He explains:

> The Church is not Catholic because she is spread abroad over the whole of the earth and can reckon on a large number of members. She was already Catholic on the morning of Pentecost, when all her members could be contained in a small room, as she was when the Arian waves seemed on the point of swamping her; she would still be Catholic if tomorrow apostasy on a vast scale deprived her of almost all the faithful. For fundamentally Catholicity has nothing to do with geography or statistics. If it is true that it should be displayed over all the earth and be manifest to all, yet its nature is not material but spiritual. *Like sanctity, Catholicity is primarily an intrinsic feature of the Church.*[2]

Here is a first vital lesson for us about what it means to be the Church. Catholicity points to a quality of life, to wholeness, not just to size. Living Catholicism too embraces that quality.

I was taught another important lesson a couple of years later as I began my theology degree and a more formal study of the Church in 1966. One day the lecturer informed us that our subject was really quite novel. The idea of studying the Church as such, its nature, was something which had only started in the previous century. Prior to that nobody had really bothered, believing that they knew what the Church was and that it could be taken for granted, like the air we breathe. Now we have to reflect on what it means to be the Church. In those days, immediately after the Second Vatican Council, the situation was still developing. A renewed understanding of the Church had been central to the Council's deliberations, but the renewal had not simply begun there.

(ii)

Twenty years before the Council, in 1943, Pope Pius XII had made a major contribution to this study when he produced his Encyclical Letter on the Church, *Mystici Corporis* (*The Mystical Body of Christ*). In the midst of the horrors of the Second World War (n. 4), with the Church being persecuted (n. 41) and the weak slaughtered (n. 92), the Pope had offered a vision of what it means to be the Church. The dominant image, as the Letter's title makes plain, is scriptural. 'That the Church is a body,' the Pope declared, 'we find asserted again and again in the Sacred Scriptures' (n. 14). And he quoted the letter to the Romans: 'Being many, we are one body in Christ.'[3] His reflections develop from that starting point. All the same, he has already identified the 'true Church of Christ' as 'the Holy, Catholic, Apostolic, Roman Church' (n.13): the vision excludes those who are not its members. So while the understanding of the Church is not itself legalistic, the way of handling the argument is. In spite of the scriptural basis, the approach was exclusivist and the structures juridical. At the time, that was only natural, but it gave rise to negative attitudes.

First, the claim that the Roman Catholic Church was exclusively the One, True Church made a search for truth elsewhere superfluous. There were no lessons to be learnt from others. This viewpoint displayed a confident triumphalism. Then, while the Pope stated explicitly that the body's mystical union with Christ is not something merely social or juridical, he nevertheless gave pride of place to legal structure, for he affirmed at once that 'the juridical grounds on which the Church rests and is built have their origin in the divine constitution given her by Christ' (n. 61); and by doing so he reinforced the tendency to legalism within the Church. And, thirdly, his ready remark that 'those who possess the sacred power in this Body must be considered primary and principal members' (n. 17), implied that the clergy enjoy a higher class of membership within the Church. The Pope spoke warmly of all the baptized, but his perspective was not only hierarchical, which is to be expected, but, more specifically, one which gave the clergy priority. At that time, these attitudes — triumphalism, legalism, and clericalism — were instinctive when thinking about the Church. They shaped the draft document on the subject which was placed before the bishops in Council on 2 December 1962. But later that morning Bishop Emile-Josef De Smedt of Bruges denounced the draft on these very grounds of triumphalism, legalism, and clericalism. He concluded, 'No mother ever spoke in this way.' Some have regarded his speech as the most effective of the session and possibly of the entire Council.[4] The great majority of bishops agreed with him. They were looking for something else. They wanted an approach which was biblical rather than legal and which sought to include people rather than exclude them.

The document on the Church which they produced two years later, *Lumen Gentium* (*The Light of the Nations*), bore those marks. Its flavour was scriptural. There was a blizzard of biblical images: the Church is a sheepfold, a field to be cultivated, a vineyard; it is God's building, his house and household, his dwelling-place and temple; and the temple is the Holy City and the New Jerusalem, being prepared like a bride adorned for her husband; the Church is Mother and spotless spouse; and there is much more.[5] Moreover, it affirmed plainly that people are incoporated into the Church through baptism and so its approach to those who are baptized, although they are not Catholics, was full of respect. Besides them, it also spoke warmly of the Jews, of Moslems, and those of other religions or none who seek to live according to the truth with integrity.[6] The central image described the Church as the People of God. It was welcomed enthusiastically. Much has already been written on this subject.

Twenty years on, however, in 1984 Fr Raymond Brown whose distinction as a scriptural scholar has been so widely recognized, was writing, 'Within Roman Catholicism, if we have another decade of the dominance of the people of God imagery, the body of Christ motif will need to re-emerge'. Here was a real challenge, because the 'body of Christ' motif tended still to be associated with the legalism of Pius XII. But Brown was not trying to retrieve that past. A little later, he explained his reason, it was 'to preserve a sense of a Church holiness that comes from Christ and goes beyond the status of the members'.[7] The concern is not for the old legalism, but to safeguard holiness, the reality within, at the heart of Christian life.

Even as he was writing, an Extraordinary Synod was in preparation. It was held the following year, 1985, to mark the twentieth anniversary of the close of the Council. It produced a short report. One sentence reads, 'The ecclesiology of communion is a central and fundamental idea in the documents of the Council.'[8] It is an intriguing remark. Turn to *Lumen Gentium* and you will find perhaps one single, shy reference to 'communion': 'Established by Christ as a communion of life, love, and truth, it [the Church] is taken up by him also as the instrument for the salvation of all.'[9] That is all. The word 'communion' is used on various other ocasions in *Lumen Gentium*, but without the depth the Synod's Report implied. What makes the remark intriguing, however, is the fact that, contrary to appearances, it is true.

The conciliar text in which the understanding of the Church as communion came into its own was *Unitatis Redintegratio*, the Decree on Ecumenism, because it allowed for a greater subtlety in speaking of the relationship between Catholics and those who were separated from them, moving beyond a straightforward distinction between union and separation and recognizing that there could be degrees of unity. The Decree declares that those 'who believe in Christ and have been truly baptized are put in some kind of communion with the Catholic Church, even though this communion is imperfect'.[10] The meaning of the phrase is clear. Even so, the specific use of the concept is slight. However, its significance has emerged. I recall Bishop Christopher Butler who, as Abbot of Downside, had attended the Council, leading an in-service training day for priests of the Shrewsbury Diocese in the mid-seventies, ten years, therefore, before this Synod, and commenting upon its growing importance. It illustrated the way an idea may be influential without at once being much noticed. He also joked about being unsure how the Greek should be pronounced: was it *koinonìa* or *koinònia*? And was it translated better as 'fellowship' or 'communion'? Neither really does it justice, but 'communion' seems now to be established. At the Extraordinary Synod its status was affirmed and since then, in the major documents which have followed the Synods on the Lay Faithful (*Christifideles Laici*) in 1987, on Priestly Formation (*Pastores Dabo Vobis*) in 1992, and on Religious Life (*Vita Consecrata*) in 1996, its significance has been fundamental and unmistakable. So what are we saying when we speak of the Church as 'communion'?

(iii)

When Catholics have spoken about communion in the past, they have usually meant 'going to holy communion', receiving the eucharist, or else they have been referring to the Church as the communion of saints, the bond between those who are in heaven, those on earth, and those in purgatory. Pope Paul VI, for example, speaking in a General Audience shortly after he had closed the Council, illustrated this use. 'The Church is a *communion*,' he said. 'In this context what does *communion* mean?' And then he answered his own question: 'The meaning of the Church is a communion of saints.'[11] The meaning which has emerged, however, has developed that teaching richly, for it sees its value as lying in its ability to link the interior life of the Church to the depths of God's life. It safeguards precisely that holiness which Raymond Brown was anxious to preseve.

It does so because communion implies and holds together

three elements which are intimately linked: it affirms the unity of all the baptized; it respects their distinctiveness; and then it deals with the relationship between this unity and distinctiveness. When people live in communion, they will have a real sense of what makes them one, while they will respect the differences which make them distinctive and separate from one another, and they will work at this combination of unity and difference by nurturing their relationships. These are the qualities which should characterize the Church. Why do they answer Brown's concern? How do they make us holy?

We need to remember what we say about our God. We believe that God is one. We also believe that in God there are three distinct Persons, the Father, the Son, and the Holy Spirit. These three Persons are not three Gods. There is only one God. The Father is God; the Son is God; and the Spirit is God. But as Persons, they are distinct from each other: the Father is not the Son or the Spirit, he was not crucified, nor did he descend on the disciples at Pentecost; the Son is not the Father or the Spirit, he was not the origin of creation nor did he descend at Pentecost; and the Spirit is not the Father or the Son, he was not the origin of creation nor was he crucified. God is one. But within the Godhead there are these three distinct Persons. And how do we give an account of this unity and distinctiveness in God? We speak of the relations between them. Basic Trinitarian theology is working with unity (there is one God), distinctiveness (there are three Persons), and relationship (to account for both unity and distinctiveness).

When we understand ourselves as Church in terms of communion – unity, distinctiveness, and relationship – then we are seeking to live our Christian life in a way that reflects the life of God and is rooted in the life of God. *Christifideles Laici* states it plainly: 'In this communion is the wonderful reflection and participation in the mystery of the intimate life of love in God as Trinity, Father, Son and Holy Spirit as revealed by the Lord Jesus.' To share in God's life is the very definition of holiness. And Pope John Paul is emphatic: *'Such communion is the very mystery of the Church'*.[12] That is why the understanding of the Church as communion safeguards that holiness about which Raymond Brown had expressed concern. And what has come to be called collaborative ministry flows naturally from it. It is the strategy which makes communion real.

(iv)

I have never met anyone who thought 'collaborative ministry' a beautiful turn of phrase. It is at best cumbersome, but it can have tragic connotations: there are graffiti which declare, 'Collaborators will be shot.' However, it remains in use because a term was needed to express something quite specific, and collaborative ministry is specific. It is not just any way of working together; in particular, it is not simply the most recent, trendy, fashionable way of speaking about the lay apostolate. That notion is entirely wrong-headed, because collaborative ministry is not to be reduced to the idea of one group within the Church, for example, the laity, working with another, as it might be ordained priests; it is about the way in which all the baptized – from the Pope to the person most recently received into the Church – work together to make communion real.

Some years ago, Pat Jones, who was then one of the Assistant General Secretaries to the Bishops' Conference of England and Wales, addressed the National Conference of Priests and described it in these terms. Speaking of the whole Church, she said:

> Most fundamentally, it means recognising the bond which unites us and commitment to the good we can achieve together, as primary. It becomes visible in the respect we show to each other because we are equal in value but different in our gifts and callings, and in our commitment to drawing out the gifts of all; it grows through working at a shared vision and shared decision-making and mutual accountability; and it needs a willingness to build real

> personal relationships, acknowledge limitations and vulnerability, and openness to facing and working through conflict.[13]

This passage is closely packed, but repays rereading and careful reflection. The essential elements are stated clearly: the bond which unites; the respect for diversity within the unity; and the nurturing of relationships. Being collaborative is that way of life which corresponds to communion.

At the same time, it is important to add that there is no opposition between the understanding of Church as communion and as hierarchy, although we have to take care to express their relationship accurately. It may help to realize that it is difficult to accommodate the recognition of the Church as communion if the idea of the Church as hierarchy becomes the organizing motif. If the Church is principally a command structure from the top down, how can we do justice to the vision of unity, diversity, and relationship which communion evokes? But the Church is plainly hierarchical. If, on the other hand, hierarchy is seen as a way of serving communion, then the two models plainly support each other. In *The Sign We Give*, the document on collaborative ministry produced by a Working Party for the Bishops' Conference of England and Wales, a happy image is used. It calls hierarchy a service to communion and then adds: 'Hierarchy is what holds communion together, rather like the membranes in a leaf.'[14]

It is not easy to make this understanding of Church and so this way of life real. When I find myself talking to people about collaborative ministry, sooner or later the conversation turns to conversion.

In another address at the same Priests' Conference, Vicky Cosstick, who at that time was working in the Religious Education Service of the Archdiocese of Southwark, indicated some of the qualities people need to make the experience of collaboration come alive.[15] Let me mention three: prayerfulness, maturity, and the readiness to lay power aside.

First, prayerfulness. We have seen already that we are called to pray constantly and that we respond by striving for that prayerfulness which means much more than simply saying prayers. It indicates a way of life.[16] There are also more particular aspects of the spiritual life which may be involved if collaborative ministry is to be effective,[17] but a commitment to prayerfulness, to taking seriously our call to grow in intimacy with God, is indispensable. And this way of life is not natural for us; we are in a foreign land; prayer is not our native language.[18]

Then, maturity. Adults may well be offended if told that they lack maturity, but I do not mean to give offence. By maturity I mean here simply the capacity to accept my own responsibilities and allow others to accept theirs. As an example, think of parents. I have worked enough in schools to know that there are some who, devoted as they may be to their children, are feckless when their young need help and guidance from them; they want the school to take over that role. And there are others who are never off the telephone, constantly badgering teachers about details which are already well in hand. It is a matter of knowing when the responsibility is yours and when it is another's. The same can be true of priests in parishes. Consider visits to those who are sick and housebound. It is obviously important work, but some priests scarcely visit at all, leaving it to eucharistic ministers, while others visit constantly and plead the demands of this work as a way of avoiding more taxing duties. When I was on supply once, a parishioner said to me, 'The sick are so lucky in this parish. Father visits them every week or fortnight.' Knowing the place and the man, I could not help wondering what was being neglected. Examples can be multiplied. How do we accept our own responsibilities and allow others to accept theirs? This question is linked closely to a third vital element in effective collaboration, the question of power and so, more particularly, the readiness to lay power aside.

We all like to be in control. It makes us feel secure. Some years ago I heard a woman being interviewed on television who, for reasons I cannot recall, had become the reluctant owner of a stud farm. I was only half-listening at this stage. But the horses had done well and she was now enjoying herself. What caught my attention was her answer to the question, 'And when did you begin to enjoy the work?' It was not when her horses started to win races. 'When I was in control,' she said. It is a natural response. But as we noted when thinking about prayer, it is less a matter of our being in control, and more one of allowing God to control us, 'Thou mastering me God!'[19] The idea of letting go, of placing ourselves in God's hands, can be inspiring. The reality can be a shock.

Some years ago, I had to speak about collaborative ministry on a number of occasions and would discuss with groups these qualities I am mentioning now. I was Director of the Religious Education Service in the Shrewsbury Diocese at the time and also parish priest at St Paul's in Hyde. Because of my diocesan responsibilities, Fr Paul O'Grady had also been appointed to the parish to care for its running day by day. As Easter approached, we discussed our plans for Holy Week and Paul suggested that there should be a single preacher for the liturgy of the triduum, Maundy Thursday, Good Friday, and Holy Saturday. He also argued that, as I was parish priest, it should be me, especially because I often had to be away. He would plan the ceremonies, I was not to worry about that, but I should preach. After further discussion, that was what we agreed. And so I found myself during those special days with nothing to do, but be prepared to preside and preach. And it was very difficult, because I was not in control. Paul and I have laughed about it since. There was I, telling people about the importance in collaboration of not being always in control, finding it so hard to put into practice.[20]

These three qualities can be considered separately, but they are connected intimately. By drawing us closer to God, prayerfulness opens us to greater knowledge of ourselves; that self-knowledge makes possible the awareness of where the frontier lies between our own responsibilities and those of others; and living that maturity calls for the readiness to lay power aside: we know when we must exercise control and when we have to relinquish it. From another point of view, we may feel that maturity and powerlessness are two ways of speaking about the same attitude and that prayerfulness is the source which nourishes it.

And there is more than an intimate connection. These qualities have something in common. None of them comes to us easily. In the sense described, none of us is naturally prayerful, mature, or at ease with loss of control. To exercise these qualities requires a change in us which may be painful. The cost may seem too great, like a dying. Some have already observed sadly that it is not a question of collaborative ministry having been tried and found wanting, but of it having been tried and found too difficult, and therefore abandoned. We must resist that temptation. There is a need for conversion. By allowing this renewal to take place in us we enter more deeply into the mystery of the Church as communion. We build the kingdom of God together. And Christ works through us. He has given us a strong image as a symbol. Jesus said, 'I am the vine, you are the branches.'[21] As we have already recognized, the force of the image lies in realizing that the grapes, which are the fruit of the vine, do not grow on the vine stem, but on its branches. In this image, the disciples are being taught that they are indispensable. The Lord will achieve his effect only through them. They are in communion with him, called to collaborate in his loving.

7

Providence and Miracles

(i)

GOD'S love for us knows no limits. That truth has run like a refrain through these reflections. Moreover, the particular wonder of that love is the way it comes to us. Although divine, it is not offered to us in extraordinary ways which might seem magical. God is not a chess master, intervening in our world by treating us as his pawns. We receive God's love within the ordinary circumstances of our human condition. That is one of the major lessons we learn from the incarnation. When Jesus was born, the Word became flesh not as some kind of bizarre, extraordinary human being, but as exactly the ordinary kind of human being we all are. That is how he is able to be our Saviour: the divine Son is one of us.

All the same, there are instances when God seems to intervene. We speak of certain moments as providential or inexplicable events as miraculous. Such talk raises immensely complex intellectual questions, which are well beyond the scope of what we can investigate here, but before we continue, let us at least pause to consider what more commonly we might mean when we refer to providence or declare some event a miracle. We can look at providence first.

(ii)

There is a well-known story of a soldier in the trenches during the First World War. Wanting a cigarette, he put one in his mouth and reached for his matches, but he dropped the box and bent down to pick it up. As he ducked, a sniper's bullet passed over him. Is that what we mean by providence? The bullet hit his friend, standing beside him. Then there was the case of the gifted but idle student who would not revise for his final examinations. Out at a party one night, he trips and breaks his ankle. With movement confined, he turns to his studies and goes on to do himself justice in his exams. Was the broken ankle providence? Or when, worn down, I pray for good weather during my summer holiday and my prayer is answered, is that a kindly providence at work? It may be a time when gardeners and farmers are desperate for rain. What do we mean by providence?

There is scope for a real dilemma here. On the one hand, a particular notion of providence would see God as intervening constantly, capable of manipulating events so that the outcome is always for the best. Whenever something favourable or fortunate occurs, someone will attribute it directly to God's constant providential care. But on the other hand, what are we to make of those situations which do not turn out for the best? If God is capable of acting in so constant and manipulative a fashion, why does he not intervene more and resolve the tragedies that overwhelm us? Why does he not bring peace to Northern Ireland, prevent a devastating earthquake in Turkey, take away the cancer that is killing my friend? Our common way of viewing providence, as God's loving care for us, when conceived as a matter of regular intervention, becomes a kind of nightmare. When divine action is withheld, is it a punishment or evidence of a God too capricious to be bothered? What is divine providence? Does it have any meaning at all?

We may be tempted at times by that conclusion, but then can be brought up short. In July 1999, I spent two weeks on supply at English Martyrs' in Wallasey, where I had been parish priest. During that fortnight Gerard Murray died. He had been the parish organist and choirmaster when I had first been in the parish as an assistant in the mid-seventies. Around new year in 1977 he had a heart attack and then a stroke and lost the power of speech. When he died, he had not spoken for almost twenty-three years. But I remember him from before that time.

There is only one other priest who has served in the parish who remembers him as other than a sick man or an invalid. But after all that time, for that brief period I was there. After he died, members of his family and other parishioners as well said to me often, 'Isn't it providential that you are here?', for I was the one who officiated at his requiem and so was able to pay tribute from my own knowledge, not only to the heroism of his long silent years, but also to his earlier zest for life. Call it coincidence. But it may also be seen as a sign of providential care that such a coincidence should have occurred. What do we mean when we speak about providence? For me it implies a plan, indicates a presence, and requires perception.

(iii)

First, the plan. Integral to the notion of providence is the sense that God has a plan for us. In a well-known passage, Newman once declared, 'God has created me to do Him some definite service; . . . I am a link in a chain, a bond of connexion between persons.'[1] God has a plan for us and at times, if only with hindsight, we may be able to detect it. There can be significant moments in our lives or people who have particular significance for us. Looking back we seem to detect a pattern. Let me offer an example. It has to be personal.

I went to boarding school at the age of eight. It was not as extraordinary in those days as it may seem now. The term I arrived, there was a new headmaster, Fr William Maher, who has been one of the key figures in my life. A man with great energy and an amazing appetite for work, he nevertheless had the precious gift, when you needed to speak to him, of making you feel that you were the only person who mattered and you had all his time and attention. I was not thinking of being a priest at that time, but when I did, that example of pastoral care was an inspiration. I make no claim to have matched it.

After school, I went at once to the English College in Rome to study for the priesthood. Within months a new rector was appointed. At that time, during the Council, many colleges in Rome had new rectors whose task was to manage a difficult period of change. Some were very dynamic, but in fact still caught in a pre-conciliar mould. They would make changes, but then it would be a matter of 'thus far and no further'. They had seen the need for certain changes and welcomed them, but their approach was essentially static. Sometimes these new men were moved on very quickly. Initial enthusiasm among their students was followed by disillusionment. But our new rector, Monsignor Leo Alston, was not that kind of man. His manner was quiet and diffident, and there were those who thought him not dynamic enough. This was the time when people were discussing co-responsibility in the Church. There was a lot of talk, but not necessarily all that much action. In fact, however, what others discussed, Leo Alston did. He listened to what we students were saying and sometimes said 'no', but sometimes would say 'yes'. There were bishops who disapproved. Some said he was allowing the students to get away with too much. But they were men for whom the Church was more hierarchy than communion. Leo Alston was teaching us about listening and discerning. I regard it as one of the great blessings of my life that he was rector while I was preparing for priesthood.

After ordination and completing my studies in Rome, I was sent to study at Oxford. For the next four years, I lived at the Catholic Chaplaincy, where Crispian Hollis, now the Bishop of Portsmouth, was chaplain, having just taken over from Fr Michael Hollings. Much has been written about Michael Hollings by other people on other occasions. He had transformed the style of life at the chaplaincy, opening it up to a wide range of people, making it an open house, and placing it, so far as was possible, at the service of the University at large. But it was not simply a social service; it was a ministry based on prayer and centred on the celebration of the eucharist. At least half-an-hour before the early mass, the chapel would be filling with people, praying quietly. They were there because they had seen Michael there. And Crispian maintained that tradition. It was a happy, intoxicating time, a wonderful initial experience of ministerial priesthood.

Now it is easy to see the presence of these three men in my life as a matter of chance. But when I consider what I have received from them, I find it hard not to detect a kindly hand at work, not coincidence but a providential pattern, a plan.

Secondly, presence. To speak of the influence of these three priests on me as a part of God's plan for me is to acknowledge God's presence. But was God ever absent? At once, we must say not. God's presence is an abiding presence, not an occasional favour. People or events which we regard as providential – like my return to the parish when Gerard Murray died – are rather the moments when the fact of that abiding presence breaks through with particular clarity. It is the outward manifestation of the perpetual presence. Plan and presence go together.

And so, thirdly, perception. If providence is really a way of speaking of God's loving presence, we may ask whether we should not be aware of it all the time. Perhaps we should, but we aren't. Life is not like that. Even those whom we love most in this world, we take for granted at times. And so with God. Some do not know him, others may ignore him, everyone sometimes neglects him. What we call providential are moments of perception when we recognize his presence. It may be an experience of first conversion or a reawakening. They are the times when we can detect the presence. God's care for us is not arbitrary; it is consistent and enduring. But recognition, detection, perception are vital. As we realized when we began these reflections, we have to be on the watch.

This understanding of providence can comfort us. The raw obstacle when we wonder about providence is the one mentioned earlier. If we are thinking in simplistic terms of providence as divine intervention, then we may be baffled or angry: if God can intervene sometimes, why doesn't he always overcome the evil that afflicts us? But, as we noticed earlier, God's power is not a form of superhuman power. He has created us out of love and respects our condition.[2] This teaching can be comforting

because it speaks to us, not of an occasional, intrusive, manipulative presence, but of one that endures in hardship and delight.
Moments which we recognize as providential, are like sacraments
of God's love; they are the times when we perceive that love
more clearly as an abiding reality.

If we can understand providence in this way, not as intervention but as a graced perception of an abiding loving presence,
how are we to understand miracles? Don't they show us God
breaking into the ordinary pattern of our condition?

(iv)

The Gospels are full of miracles. Jesus gives sight to the blind,
hearing and speech to the deaf and dumb; he makes the lame
walk; he cleanses lepers, casts out devils, and raises the dead; he
calms the storm and walks on water; he feeds the five thousand
and changes water into wine. These actions, as presented, defy
natural explanation. But sometimes there may in fact be such an
explanation. Perhaps those said to be possessed by Satan were in
fact mentally ill or suffering from a personality disorder which
was overcome by the calming presence of Jesus. Was the leprosy
cleansed always Hansen's Disease or a simpler skin disease which
could be cured by a greater care for hygiene? Were the accounts
of feeding the five thousand in desert places less like reports of
what actually took place, but rather composed to echo the stories
of manna in the wilderness and help the people to see Jesus as
the new Moses? There have always been people who have sought
to explain away Jesus' miracles. And the accounts we have vary
greatly. The Fourth Gospel does not speak of miracles at all, but
rather of signs, and these signs from the changing of water into
wine at the wedding feast of Cana to the raising of Lazarus have
been seen to give the first part of that Gospel its structure.
Moreover, Jesus himself seems to have been almost indifferent
to miracles. We are told that he dismissed those who looked for
signs as 'an evil and adulterous generation'.[3] He did not use
miracles to establish his position. They were not intended to

satisfy people's curiosity or desire for magic.[4] Instead, they confirmed teaching and were performed in response to faith. Where faith was slight, miracles were few.[5]

Miracles are controversial. The development of modern science has looked at the world as a system which is to be explained according to its own terms and not by appeal to external interference, and various schools of philosophy hold positions which dovetail with that view: they can give no place to supernatural intervention and regard belief in miracles as the refuge of the credulous and a cover for ignorance. The common Christian view unsurprisingly argues to the contrary that, as God is the creator or first cause of all that is, it is more probable than not that he would at times intervene in his creation, acting directly and without the use of secondary causes. And there is a further, more complex position. It takes the incarnation with utter seriousness. If the supreme revelation of the divine presence in our midst – and so its pattern – was realized in and through Jesus of Nazareth as an ordinary human being, then it may be said to be unlikely that God's action in our world would occur by a disruption of nature; it would instead take place in accordance with its normal laws. This viewpoint should not become a cover for explaining miracles away, but it should warn us against a presumption that we know precisely what is normality and what are its laws. Extraordinary events appear at times to happen. How are they to be explained? What status should we give them?

Two stories. The first was told by Michael Hollings about Padre Pio, the saintly Franciscan, recently beatified, who for fifty years bore in his own body the five wounds of the crucified Jesus and about whom many stories of wonders circulated. As a student in Rome, Michael would sometimes visit Padre Pio at San Giovanni Rotondo and serve his mass. On one occasion after mass, people said to him, 'Did you see the miracle, the miracle?' 'What miracle?' Michael asked, unaware that anything out of the ordinary had occurred. 'The host,' they said to him. 'Father held it up and then it just vanished.' But Michael had to explain that the host had simply slipped from the friar's wounded hands into the chalice. Where there is a reputation for working wonders, stories gather. Some, like this one, may be explained quite simply, but others are not.[6]

The second story was told me by Mia Woodruff, widow of Douglas Woodruff, who was for many years editor of *The Tablet*. As a young woman she was working on a pilgrimage in Lourdes, as she usually did, and one year amongst those in her care was a nun from Limoges who was suffering from tubercular peritonitis. She could scarcely eat or move and was close to death. On this particular morning she was taken down on her stretcher to the Grotto by other pilgrims. Mia remained behind, working in the hospital. At mid-morning, a friend came back from the Grotto and told her, 'I think your nun has died.' 'I don't think so,' Mia replied. 'They would have brought her back, if she had.' At lunchtime, the group returned and there was the nun, not dead, but sitting up on her stretcher, talking animatedly. Mia said to her laconically, 'They told me you'd died.' 'No,' came the reply, 'but I thought I was going to. I could feel myself going. Then I felt a kind of thrill and a voice seemed to say to me, "Get up." So I did. I sat up and now I feel fine.' She then ate a hearty lunch. The religious congregation to which she belonged was a nursing order. She returned to work in their hospital in Limoges and died years later from a cause completely unrelated to her peritonitis. Remarkable events do occur. What can they teach us?

It is perfectly reasonable to believe that God can intervene in creation. It is natural to identify exceptional and otherwise inexplicable events with such action. But we need to be cautious. What may seem inexplicable to one generation may become obvious to the next. It is not for the Church to declare, for example, what is or is not medically possible. And – as with providence – if we are not careful, miracles can seem petty. If God intervened to cure that nun in the Grotto at Lourdes that morning, why not the whole gathering? What made her special? And why stop at personal illness? Why not cure international terrorism, ethnic hatred, and natural disasters? And so we could go on. Let us return to the central theme of these reflections.

We have been created by God out of love to live in accordance with love, but we have rejected his plan for us. That rejection is sin. But God's love for us is without limit and relentless. He is the hound of heaven, he pursues us without tiring. He uncovers his love for us in so many ways and particularly in the call of Abraham and the history of the Jews and then, as we believe, by sending Jesus his Son to reveal his love to us supremely. We are invited to recognize that love, respond to it, and be faithful to it. It is not easy to do. But perhaps miracles are to be seen as those occasions, akin to providential moments, when God's love breaks through to us. It may be that miracles are exceptional, not because our usual system is being wrenched askew, but because our world's instinct is still to resist love: miracles are privileged, sacramental events, when that resistance is cracked open a little and God's love is revealed. The nun healed at Lourdes was not the only one God loved that day, while the rest were ignored: her cure was a sign and reminder to them all, whatever their condition, that they were held in his love.

(v)

There are many subtle questions surrounding belief in God's providence and miracles. Philosophers, scientists, and theologians can debate them. Their complexities need not delay us. Whatever their more technical conclusions, it is at least enough for us to recognize in these matters moments when God's overwhelming love is brought home to us more clearly either as a providential abiding presence or as a particular sign. God loves us. He calls us to answer love with love. He invites us to share his life.

8

Holiness and Discipleship

(i)

GOD invites us to share his life. Such an invitation takes our breath away. It is a call to holiness and this call has roots deep in our tradition: we remember the account in the Book of Leviticus when the Lord spoke to Moses and said, 'Say to all the congregation of the people of Israel, You shall be holy; for I the Lord your God am holy.'[1] Here is a declaration to astonish us. It concerns something far more profound than moral goodness; holiness is the code word we use for the inner life of God. We cannot describe that inner life, and so we say, God is holy. And we are called to become holy as the Lord our God is holy. How can we respond to that call? We must pray, of course; we seek to come close to God; but our lives must also reflect our share in God's life. How can they? What are we to do? What guidance are we offered? I find help by turning to the Sermon on the Mount.

Our Scriptures are full of sayings which offer us powerful challenges, but few can compare with Jesus' command, 'Be perfect, therefore, as your heavenly Father is perfect.' The summons to perfection may seem even more demanding than the call to holiness. And I wonder how many people down the Christian generations have felt overwhelmed by a sense of their own inadequacy and even guilt, as they have realized how incapable they were of obeying it. It seems impossible. It is. Which of us can claim to match the Father's perfection? So we are all failures. Or maybe we have missed the key word. The key word is 'therefore'. The saying is as much a conclusion as a command. It draws together teaching about loving enemies as well as friends, inspired by awareness that God's love embraces everyone. Jesus is reminding us that the heavenly Father 'makes his sun rise on the evil and the good, and sends rain on the righteous and the unrighteous'.[2] This perfection is not an abstract ideal; it refers specifically to the way we treat people in the ordinary circumstances of each day, whoever they may be, those we find easy and those we do not. Do we treat them equally, which is the way God treats us? I love the apocryphal story of the old passing stranger whom Abraham entertained generously, but who behaved rudely. When questioned, he showed contempt for Abraham's God. Abraham threw him out.

> When the old man was gone, God called to Abraham and asked him where the stranger was. He replied: 'I thrust him away because he did not worship thee.' God answered him: 'I have suffered him these hundred years, although he dishonoured me; and couldst thou not endure him one night?'[3]

That is the perfection in view here. Do we only love those who love us or can we open our hearts wider to include those whom we dislike? That is the lesson Jesus is teaching and it points to a more general lesson still. It shows us that the holiness and perfection to which we are called are interwoven inextricably with action. The way we live has to reflect the reality deep inside us. God loves us and calls us to answer love with love. Living Catholicism is a call to share God's life, to become holy, and it must be put into practice. It has to reveal itself in the way we live our lives, which are to be lives inspired by that very divine presence within us which shows itself in the way we love God and one another. That is discipleship in action.

To understand better the implications of this connection between holiness and discipleship, we can learn from three successive Gospel conversations: when Jesus spoke to the rich young man, when he answered the ambitions of the sons of Zebedee, and when he cured Bartimaeus.[4]

(ii)

If the Lord's words in the Sermon on the Mount about perfection have caused anguish, how much more heart-searching has there been over his words to the rich young man? Once again, it is the word 'perfect' which captures our attention. In St Matthew's account we are told that Jesus invited him to become a disciple with the words, 'If you wish to be perfect, go, sell your possessions and give the money to the poor, and you will have treasure in heaven; then come, follow me.' But the young man could not accept the invitation. He 'went away grieving, for he had many possessions.'[5] We can sympathize. We do not need to have much ourselves to be aware how limited our own response is when judged by this standard. But shouldn't we too be seeking perfection?

However, perhaps the extreme character of the demand Jesus makes of this man should put us on our guard. First of all, it helps to realize that this command does not apply automatically to everyone. A little earlier in Mark's Gospel, for example, Jesus has healed the man who says his name is Legion, because he is possessed by many demons. And afterwards, as Jesus was leaving, we are told that this man, now cured, 'begged him that he might be with him'. These are strong and beautiful words. If the invitation to the rich young man had automatic, universal application, Jesus could not have refused. But he did. He told him instead, 'Go home to your friends, and tell them how much the Lord has done for you, and what mercy he has shown you.'[6] And the man obeyed him. He went away and proclaimed how much Jesus had done for him. So the way to perfection offered to the rich man is not for everyone. This incident teaches us that the path to holiness and discipleship can take different directions. We ought to examine more closely this conversation between Jesus and this rich young man who approached him.

The man asks Jesus what he must do to inherit eternal life. That is what he wants. Jesus tells him to keep the commandments, not to murder, steal, commit adultery, and the rest. He replies, 'I have kept all these; what do I still lack?' And then, as we have seen, Jesus invites him to be a disciple, saying, 'If you wish to be perfect', go and sell, come and follow. He is not uttering an abstract command, to be applied without qualification to everyone. When we see the invitation in context, we see that it is a particular request made to this person. He is a man with high ideals. In the Marcan Gospel, we are told that, when he claimed to have kept the commandments, Jesus looked at him and loved him. So we may presume it was not an idle boast. He won Jesus' admiration. But there was a flaw in him. He assumed that, because he kept the commandments, nothing was beyond him, he could achieve whatever was asked of him. So Jesus punctured his conceit. The rich young man wished to be perfect, but not in fact at any price. His desire was qualified by his care for his possessions and, when he was put to the test, they mattered to him more. He walked sorrowfully away. Jesus had challenged him.

Those who wish to be disciples will find that they are challenged as well: they will have to come to terms with their own weaknesses. Some years ago, friends of mine told me a story. A man they know was driving his vintage Bentley in London on a fine summer's day. He stopped at the traffic lights and another car drew up alongside. The driver of the second car rolled down his window and admired the Bentley. The man said, 'When the lights change, I'll meet you over the road.' They parked and talked and, to cut the story short, ended by exchanging cars. I mention the incident because I don't suppose that, if the rich man had had the same attitude to his possessions as this man had to his vintage Bentley, he would have been tested in the way he was. Jesus challenged him by exposing his weakness. He showed him how much his wealth meant to him. But had his attitude been the same, he would still have been tested. All disciples are. Jesus searches us out.

And so the question comes to us: what price do we place upon discipleship? Are we like this rich young man, confident until tested? Will we follow Jesus provided we have peace of mind and our popularity is undiminished, provided our career is successful and our life at home contented, provided our health is good and our standard of living secure? The list could be continued. All these things are good and to be valued, but what is their importance for us? Are they the conditions which qualify our commitment? Are we pleased to live a devoted Christian life when content, but soon disenchanted when crisis strikes? The conversation with the rich young man is teaching us two lessons: first, that, if we wish to be disciples, we will be tested, our weaknesses will be exposed; and secondly, that our commitment must be unconditional.

The very idea of unconditional commitment may alarm us. From one point of view, it should: following Christ is not a trivial pursuit. So we need to consider carefully what it entails.

When the young man had gone, Jesus reflected further on the incident with his disciples and underlined the lesson: 'Truly, I say to you, it will be hard for a rich man to enter the kingdom of heaven. Again I tell you, it is easier for a camel to go through the eye of a needle than for a rich man to enter the kingdom of God.'[7] This teaching takes the disciples by surprise. Jesus is using hyperbole to make his point. 'What is the largest animal you can think of?' he is saying. They answer, 'A camel.' 'And the smallest hole?' 'The eye of a needle.' 'Very good. It is easier to get that great beast through that tiny hole than for someone who is rich to get into heaven.' They are amazed. We see their amazement in their response. They do not ask simply, 'How can anyone who is rich be saved?', but, 'Then who can be saved?' For them, wealth like health was a sign of God's favour. If the rich who are favoured have such difficulty, how can anyone at all, they wonder, be saved? And they are taught that what is impossible for us is possible for God. We are not saved by our own efforts. Salvation is a gift from God. We must place ourselves in his hands; we must rely on him. Both holiness and discipleship require that trust. It is fundamental. Lives built on trust make commitment unconditional.

But we may still feel alarmed. Will unconditional commitment mean enclosed monasteries for all? We need to remember again what we have learnt through Jesus' conversation with the rich young man. The invitation he received, go and sell, come and follow, was offered for a particular purpose, to challenge *him*. But devoted discipleship can take many forms. Perhaps no one has expressed that truth more eloquently than St Francis de Sales. Everyone, he taught, must seek perfection, but the way it is done will differ depending upon who they are and the method chosen 'must be accommodated to their particular strength, circumstances and duties'. As he observed, 'If workmen spent as much time in church as religious, if religious were exposed to the same pastoral calls as a bishop, such devotion would be ridiculous and cause intolerable disorder.'[8] Times have changed since the beginning of the seventeenth century, but the principle remains valid.

The conversation with the rich young man lays the foundations for discipleship: we have to confront our weaknesses or a genuine commitment can never be made. Peter seems shocked and asks a characteristic question. He wonders about his own position and that of the other disciples who have left everything and followed Jesus: 'What then will we have?' Jesus reassures him: they will be judges of Israel, and all who have left home and family and possessions for his sake will receive back a hundred times over what they have given up and – it was the desire of the rich young man – they will inherit eternal life. However, in the Marcan account he strikes a warning note as well: there would be persecutions.[9]

(iii)

A brief interlude follows. Jesus speaks to the Twelve about the suffering he would have to endure. Then, shortly afterwards, he is approached by the sons of Zebedee, James and John.

They are brimful of confidence. Their brash demand clashes with the more sombre mood which is gathering in the Gospel. They say: 'Teacher, we want you to do for us whatever we ask of you.' I always imagine his reply to have been made in a rather soft tone of voice. It should have put them on their guard, but it does not. They seem too absorbed with their own concerns. He asks, 'What do you want me to do for you?' And they plunge on. Have they been enthused by the notion of being judges of Israel? They say, 'Grant us to sit, one at your right hand and one at your left, in your glory.' But he deflects them from power and reminds them of persecution: 'You do not know what you are asking. Are you able to drink the cup that I drink, or be baptized with the baptism that I am baptized with?' Their confidence is undiminished. They declare: 'We are able.' And Jesus promises them that they shall share his cup and be baptized with his baptism, although the place at his right and left hand is not in his gift, 'it is for those for whom it has been prepared.'[10] The favoured sons of Zebedee who had with Peter seen him transfigured and were later to witness more closely his agony in the garden, are being taught that closeness to Jesus brings not comfort, but the cross. It is a further lesson in discipleship. First, the Lord seeks out our weak spot and exposes our vulnerability and then, as we come to know ourselves better, he teaches us the cost of discipleship. It was a lesson the brothers came to learn.

According to a tradition, all the apostles were put to death, except John. So James suffered like the rest, but John lived on into old age, proclaiming the fundamental gospel message, 'Little children, love one another.'[11] Thinking about that tradition, I have sometimes wondered how hard that long life must have been for him. Was it a relief or a burden? What was it like to be the last to be left from such a company? Was he pleased to be spared so that he could continue his ministry or did he ask himself whether he was somehow unworthy to make the ultimate sacrifice? Perhaps there was something of both. But the Lord's words were fulfilled: in their different ways both drank the cup and received the baptism. They discovered the cost of intimacy with Jesus and the cost of discipleship. And there is a cost for us. Servants are not greater than the master.

We thought earlier about the sufferings of Jesus. He suffered physically, personally, and spiritually. He was put to the test. These sufferings, we saw, were a consequence of his loving; they were not a form of training. He was not like an athlete going through the pain barrier to win the prize. I remember hearing once of a runner who trained with a cricket roller strapped to his back. He kept on pushing himself harder so that he would be able to run faster. Whatever truth there may be in the saying, 'No gain without pain', it has no bearing on Jesus' experience. He did not suffer in order to improve the results of his ministry. He loved, but was broken. He died with his mission in disarray and his cause apparently defeated. But he had remained faithful to his calling, faithful in love. He was broken on the cross, but rose in glory.

Holiness is a vocation to love which is a way of life. It is the very heart of discipleship. If we are faithful to this vocation, we find that it not only affects our interior disposition, but that it also creates a readiness to accept its own consequences. Belief and action are in tune. The experience may be one of brokenness. There will be sacrifices we have to make. It is not something we seek as a path to success; we may be losing what seems to us most precious. The rich young man could not bear to part with his possessions.

This teaching must be taken seriously. Christian discipleship demands cross-bearing. Sometimes it leads to loss of life, to martyrdom. But often, more prosaically, it is the one burden we feel we cannot possibly carry. When we say to the Lord, 'Anything but that', meaning, for example, the breakdown of a marriage, the death of someone we love, the affliction with some physical handicap, long periods of depression, the frustration of cherished plans, whatever it may be, he seems to reply, 'But that is what I want from you.' It is the very sacrifice he asks. And it may not be one major crisis, but a series of demands which drain us as the years pass. The life of Newman seems to me to illustrate this experience very clearly. Year by year, he remained faithful, but the demands made upon him tested him to the limit. He came to know the cost of discipleship drop by drop.

He was almost ninety when he died, a Cardinal, held in high regard by countless people, but his life had not always been like that. His early life was devoted to championing the Catholic tradition within the Church of England, but his hopes were overturned. His reception into the Catholic Church brought about a terrible parting from many of his dearest friends; after seventeen years one of them, John Keble, wrote him a moving letter, asking his forgiveness for the long silence.[12] And then, for many years as a Catholic, Newman kept receiving invitations to use his considerable gifts in ways which could have been deeply satisfying for him and beneficial to the Church, only to find the offers sabotaged. He was asked to found a university in Dublin and did so, but his efforts were constantly being thwarted. He was asked to translate the Bible and made plans, but the invitation dissolved: his work was undermined by lack of support. He was asked to edit a Catholic periodical, *The Rambler*, but then almost at once encouraged to resign. His hopes of returning to Oxford by establishing a house there were systematically frustrated. He knew himself to be an object of pity and contempt. It comes as no surprise to find this entry in his Journal in 1863:

> O how forlorn and dreary has been my course since I have been a Catholic! . . . since I made the great sacrifice to which God called me, he has rewarded me in ten thousand ways, O how many! but he has marked my course with almost unintermittent mortification . . . since I have been a Catholic, I seem to myself to have had nothing but failure, personally.[13]

Newman's experience is one example of the way the cost of discipleship need not be concentrated in a single dramatic ordeal, but may be something gradual. Nor was he exceptional. I suspect that many people can confirm that. Whatever form it takes, spectacular or unseen, the cost of discipleship is high: there is a cup to be drunk, a baptism with which to be baptized, a sacrifice to be made. But what are we called to do as disciples when we have recognized the price that must be paid? What is asked of us? It is time to turn to Bartimaeus.

(iv)

There is a natural link between the conversation Jesus had with Bartimaeus and his conversation with the sons of Zebedee. When blind Bartimaeus was sitting by the roadside on the outskirts of Jericho and realized that it was Jesus who was passing, so that he called out and was brought to Jesus, Jesus asked him the very same question he had put to James and John: 'What do you want me to do for you?' But Bartimaeus makes no brash demand. He replies simply: 'Master, let me receive my sight.' And his wish is granted: 'Go your way; your faith has made you well.' And we are told that he received his sight immediately and followed him on the way.[14] James and John, intimates of Jesus, had not understood his purpose; they sought a place in an earthly kingdom; they were ambitious for power; while the blind man saw more clearly than those with sight that the Son of man 'came not to be served but to serve'.[15] Bartimaeus goes to Jesus for a service and those who wish to be disciples must be like Bartimaeus, recognizing him for who he is, approaching him humbly, and placing themselves in his hands. We are not the source of the service we offer. This costly discipleship involves, first of all, a service which we receive; it is offered as invitation, as gift. Then like Bartimaeus we seek to offer it to others by following Jesus on the way.

Discipleship means service. We will consider later the implications of that apparently simple conclusion.[16] For the moment we can return to the Book of Leviticus with which we began. Here we notice how the source of that service is to be found in holiness. Holiness and discipleship are woven together inextricably.

We remember the words: 'Say to all the congregation of the people of Israel, You shall be holy; for I the Lord your God am holy.'[17] We feel overwhelmed. As we asked at the beginning, how can we aspire to the very holiness of God? But the answer lies where it lay before, by being attentive to its setting. As it was important not to read Jesus' teaching about perfection in isolation, so it is important to read this saying about holiness in context. After instructions about reverence for parents, the rejecting of idols, and the manner of sacrifice, there is a substantial passage which commands care for the poor and the passer-by, for those who are employed and those who are disabled, and denounces injustice, theft, lying, and corruption. And each section concludes with the refrain: 'I am the Lord.' The holiness held up to us is displayed in the just service of others, indeed virtually identified with it, and it is summed up by the words which Jesus will make part of the great commandment: 'You shall love your neighbour as yourself.'[18]

The same lesson is found in St Matthew's Gospel in the parable of the sheep and the goats. We know it well. It is an image of judgement. Entrance into the kingdom or condemnation do not depend upon the achievement of some abstract ideal of holiness or perfection, but again upon making service real in our lives. Have we fed the hungry and given drink to the thirsty, welcomed the stranger, clothed the naked, and visited those who are sick or in prison? The lesson seems to echo the teaching of Leviticus, but there is a difference, for the motive here is not found in loving others as ourselves, but in loving them as Christ. By giving or failing to give them service, we offer or fail to offer service to the Son of man: 'as you did it . . . [or] did it not to one of the least of these, you did it . . . [or] did it not to me.'[19] All the same, these two motives are not entirely distinct. A kind of equation is offered to us.

The command to love others as we love ourselves may be based at one level on practical wisdom. A reasonable degree of self-knowledge makes us aware of our weaknesses as well as our strengths, so we do not make unreal demands of ourselves and we make allowances for our failures. Those qualities are good and offer us helpful criteria for our treatment of others. But

Christian self-knowledge goes deeper. As Christian men and women, the seed of Christ's life has been sown in us to transform the very depths of our being. It has been the central theme of these pages: Jesus came to overcome our resistance to the Father's love by revealing that love through his own faithful loving, in all circumstances, even to his dying on the cross; because he was faithful, he was raised from the dead and we and all those who believe in him have become much more than his admirers and imitators: we have received his Spirit, been formed into a people as his body, the Church, and so have been brought to share in his life. We 'are the body of Christ and individually members of it.'[20] Our lives should reflect his. In others words, we must try to show others that unreserved love which we have received from him. Here is holiness and here is the equation: the service which is the fruit of holiness and which makes us disciples, becomes real when the Christ-life which has been nurtured in us, recognizes the life of Christ present in others. Then to say that I love and serve my neighbour as myself is to say that I love and serve my neighbour as the Christ.

(v)

The three conversations we have considered have shown us that the path to true discipleship, inspired by holiness, is a demanding one. When Jesus spoke to the rich young man, he exposed his weakness, he stripped away his illusions about himself. We must expect no less. Those who wish to follow Jesus have to know themselves and trust in God. Our commitment must be un-conditional. That is the only way to get a camel through the eye of a needle. When he spoke to James and John, he made plain to them that discipleship is costly: those who follow will have to make sacrifices. And when he spoke to Bartimaeus and cured him, he praised his faith: he had overcome the discourage-ment from the crowd and placed himself without reserve in Jesus' hands. If we want to be his disciples, we must face our own vulnerability, give without counting the cost, and build our lives on faith. It is a daunting prospect.

We ask how we can possibly measure up to it. It is a natural question. We know that we are flawed and weak. So before we reflect upon the implications of this vocation and how we can put it into practice, we should pause. Help is at hand. We can feed on the bread of life and be strengthened; we can acknowledge our flaws and be reconciled.

9

Eucharist and Reconciliation

(i)

GOD lavishes his love on us. It has been our constant theme. We have seen that he invites us to share his life, that is, to be holy, by being disciples of Jesus, his Son. We recognize that this invitation lies at the very heart of living Catholicism: God takes the initiative and calls us. And we are amazed, because we know from our own experience how feeble our response is. We know we are not perfect. Sometimes in confession a person will say, 'It is at least a year since I last came to confession, Father.' The voice is a little tense. There is a pause, quite a long pause. I don't want to barge in too briskly; I must allow the person to compose himself. Then I say, 'And what is it you want to mention to me?' This time the pause is briefer and he says, 'I don't know, Father. I can't think of anything.' I might then ask, 'So you've been perfect, have you?' The tension breaks, the laughter comes, and the acknowledgement, 'Well, no.' And we can continue to celebrate the sacrament. We know that we are not perfect.

We all fall short in love; indeed, we erect barriers against love; that is what we mean by sin. We should not imagine, however, that God is playing tricks on us. He has not offered us this invitation to share his life, but denied us the means of accepting it. In particular, he shows us his love through the sacraments. They are his acts of love for us. Although God is spirit, his love for us is not exclusively spiritual, engaging only the spiritual dimension of our nature. He loves us as we are, not only as he is, and we are physical as well as spiritual beings: when we love, we express our love in word and action, we tell people we love them, we hold and kiss them. The wonder of God's love for us is the way he respects our condition. The sacraments reflect that. They celebrate God's love for us in word and gesture. And while people are baptized and confirmed and, as may be, ordained only once, and the sick are anointed rarely, at the beginning of an illness or when their condition is critical, and a second marriage will occur only in special circumstances, we are encouraged to celebrate the sacraments of the eucharist and of reconciliation regularly and, in the case of the eucharist, even daily. Through these two sacraments God nurtures the Christ-life within us during the ordinary course of our lives. They are meant to sustain us, to support us in holiness and discipleship. We will consider them in turn.

(ii)

Eucharist

In the eucharist Christ feeds us. We do not suppose that he nourishes his life in us only on those occasions. The sweep of these reflections has brought us to recognize that he loves us constantly and unfailingly. But in the eucharist that love is expressed in an outstanding way. Here we celebrate and receive the nourishment we need in order to grow in holiness and be faithful in discipleship. At mass the drama of our redemption is made really present to us. We must return to a familiar theme.

God created us out of love; we exist for no other reason; we have been loved by God into existence. That love allowed us freedom, for love is not coercive. Being free, we then chose to resist love. As we have seen, that is what we mean by sin: the root of sin is the rejection of love. But such was God's love for us that he longed for the love between himself and us to be restored. He approached us in many ways, but particularly through the people of Israel as his chosen people he sought to reveal his faithful love for us. And finally, as we believe, in Jesus of Nazareth he sent his Son. The Word of God became flesh and dwelt amongst us. Jesus revealed the Father's unreserved love for us by his own unreserved love. He loved us and accepted the consequences of that loving, whatever they might be. And his love was revealed most clearly in his acceptance of suffering and there was no extreme of suffering – physical, personal, spiritual – he would not undergo for our sakes. And his suffering and the love it revealed were displayed for us supremely on the cross.[1] At every mass we stand once more, so to speak, at the foot of the cross to contemplate the love that the Father through Jesus never fails to offer us.

But how can that be possible? How can we return in time to stand on Calvary? To answer that question, I find it helps to look afresh at the way we understand memory, time, and words.

First of all, memory. Memory for us is usually passive. We recall a past event, perhaps something happy from when we were young. We remember it with pleasure and, over the years, tell the story with increasing nostalgia. Memory is passive. But not always. For example, people sometimes erect memorials, not only to stop others forgetting the past, but also to make the past present. Driving once through Israel I realized suddenly that the memorials there served that purpose. They were meant to take hold of the past and bring it into the present. It is a natural part of Jewish culture. Memory can be active and the celebration of Passover illustrates that clearly. When Jesus said, 'Do this as a memorial of me', he was drawing on that rich attitude.

And then there is time. Again, we normally think of time as measuring seconds, minutes, hours, days, weeks, months, years, and so on. Time is quantitative, a measurement. But for the Jews it is more important that time is qualitative: there is a kind of time and we need to recognize it. Remember the famous passage from Ecclesiastes which begins, 'For everything there is a season, and a time for every matter under heaven: a time to be born and a time to die, a time to plant, and a time to pluck up what is planted . . .'[2] And there are in fact situations in which we recognize time as something qualitative. It does not only measure the period within which events take place; it also tells us what kind of events they are. When someone who is in difficulties is suddenly blessed by good fortune, we may say, 'He thought all his Christmases had come at once.' There is a kind of time which is, for example, Christmastime, which we acknowledge in a particular way.

And then, finally, there are words. We commonly regard words as descriptive, their function as static. But words are not always static; they can be dynamic, creative. When Americans say, 'Have a nice day', that is their wish and hope for you; when God says, 'Have a nice day', you have a nice day, there is no question about it. When God said, 'Let there be light', there was light. God's blessings make real what they proclaim. At the Last Supper, when Jesus took the bread and the cup and he said, 'This is my body, this is my blood', then those elements became indeed his body and blood. And when the priest, by virtue of the power of his ordination, speaks the narrative of institution at mass, then once more bread and wine become the body and blood of Christ. These words are designated words, instinct with power. They effect what they proclaim.

When we recognize that memory can be active as well as passive, that time can possess a quality, not merely supply a measurement, and that words can make real what they proclaim, and when we realize that every mass is such an active memorial in a particular time, using words filled with power, we can come to see how each mass is not a repetition of Calvary, but gathers us on every occasion at the foot of the cross. We are always there. To take part in the mass, to hear the Word proclaimed and to receive the eucharist, is to be caught up in the intimate depths of love at the very core of living Catholic faith: here Jesus reveals love and offers it to us and indeed in a way which unveils the future as well; we anticipate the heavenly banquet. We are invited, even day by day, to take part, so as to be strengthened and sustained in our vocation to holiness and discipleship.

We must take part. Our participation is vital, but talk of sharing can be deeply off-putting for some people. It can be identified with an extrovert superficiality which makes some of us recoil. Tastes and styles and situations vary; we can allow for the fact that different people will feel at home in different settings, but participation is not optional, it is essential. So we need to be clear about what it involves.

Years ago I heard Richard Burton being interviewed. On being asked what for him would be the best possible setting for acting, he replied it would be on stage, not making a film or appearing on television, and he added, 'before an audience of about two hundred people who understood what was going on.' And I thought at once that that is like liturgy. Occasionally there may be a performance in rehearsal which is outstanding, but essentially the play is not just a matter of the players on stage: an attentive audience has an integral part to play in the drama. And liturgy is not only what takes place in the sanctuary; an attentive congregation is essential to the celebration. The kind of participation may vary, perhaps much song, perhaps much silence, depending on the occasion, but participation is essential.

When we receive the eucharist, we are brought to a share in Christ's life and nourished by that life in a way that should inspire wonder in us. As Herbert McCabe once remarked, 'There is a difference in kind between a gift of food and any other gift. If I give you a cigarette or a new tie I am giving you something that will please you, but when I pass you the potatoes I am giving you life.'[3] To be given food is to be given life. To be given this food which is the body and blood of Christ is to be given his life. That is what should stir wonder in us. Jesus was a man possessed by love who wanted everyone to be as possessed by love as he was. By dying on the cross and at his resurrection, he revealed that love to us, offered it to us, and made it possible for us to be as possessed by it as he was. It is this life and this overwhelming love that we share in sacramentally in the eucharist.[4] He feeds us. But still we fail and fall short in love. As well as this food, we are offered a particular path to forgiveness and healing.

(iii)

Reconciliation

By the sacrament of reconciliation our sins are forgiven and our life in Christ is renewed, but it is commonplace to hear people remark on the decline in practice of individual confession at present. There are many reasons for it. Some will feel that the words and formulae learnt and used since they were children – 'I have forgotten my morning prayers, I have quarrelled, I have told lies' – do not capture suitably the complexities of adult life, and they are right, but they don't know what other words to use; some will have had bad experiences, when they have felt more judged than reconciled; some again, particularly as they grow older, feel embarrassed by the admission of their failings; and some too will feel that they can ask God for forgiveness without approaching a priest. Many other reasons could be given. I have suggested these because they cluster around a general sense of unease which people may have, an unease which in turn leads them no longer to appreciate what this sacrament has to offer. That appreciation needs to be rekindled.

One place to begin is with the comment about God forgiving us without our needing to approach a priest. We should recognize the sense in which that is correct. Please do not misunderstand what I am saying. I am not wishing to undervalue the importance of the sacrament. The point to grasp is that God does not forgive us our sins only when we go to confession. I am not just referring to the fact that the sacraments of baptism and eucharist also confer forgiveness. It is rather a question of remembering that forgiving is a part of loving. They are linked inextricably and not confined only to those occasions when an apology is being made and accepted. When we truly love someone, but have fallen out with them, instinctively we seek to be reconciled. We want to heal the hurt that separates us. We believe that it is the same with God. His steadfast love for us is alive with the desire for us to be forgiven; to put it in other words, because he loves us, God longs for us to be saved from our sins, to be reconciled to him. And while the sacrament of reconciliation is not the only channel of that forgiveness, it is a privileged channel. 'Love means never having to say you are sorry' was the vapid soundbite used to promote a sentimental film some years ago. But when we offend those whom we love, the very thing we want most is the means and opportunity to apologize, to say we are sorry. As we have realized, God's way of loving us corresponds to our condition. The sacrament of reconciliation offers a setting in which we can actually say we are sorry for our sins, receive God's pardon and peace, and so be reconciled.

It is wonderful to be forgiven, but also mysterious. I find some words of Sheila Cassidy's capture the sense of wonder for me. Prompted in part by the torture she suffered in Chile, she once wrote: 'Frankly, I do not understand about forgiveness. I only know that it is something very holy and very healing and it is quite simply a gift of God.'⁵ It is a great impoverishment of our Christian lives for so wonderful a gift to be used rarely. It diminishes us because, when we seek forgiveness, we may release within us a capacity for love of which we had been unaware; when we do not, we may keep that love trapped inside us.

Remember the woman in St Luke's Gospel who seems to have gatecrashed the dinner to which Jesus has been invited by Simon the Pharisee. She washes Jesus' feet with her tears and dries them with her hair; she kisses them and anoints them. Simon protests at Jesus' allowing such behaviour because the woman has the reputation of being a sinner. But Jesus commends her and tells Simon that 'her sins, which are many, are forgiven, for she loved much'.⁶ People have disagreed about what that saying means, but it cannot mean that her sins are permitted because she has loved. Jesus is not allowing her to sin and go on sinning, simply because she has at the same time a kindly disposition. He is rather indicating to Simon that her sins have in fact been forgiven. How does he know? Because of the love that she is showing. When our sins are forgiven, we release love into our lives. The link between love and forgiveness is intimate, but it can also be a strain.

We discover here a significant obstacle to celebrating this sacrament. Forgiveness can only be exercised when there has been wrongdoing. One person is late for a vital appointment because taken sick, another because too idle to arrive on time. Only the second needs forgiveness; the first is the victim of circumstances beyond his control. Two cars in separate incidents crash and kill a bystander. The first was being driven with great care but tragically skidded on black ice; the second was being driven at high speed and went out of control; again, only the second needs to be forgiven and for the same reason. Before we can receive forgiveness, we need to be able to acknowledge that we have done wrong, that we are at fault. We may find that hard; it can be a strain; but like the man at the beginning of this chapter we know we are not perfect. There is evil in our world and we know we have to take some responsibility for it.

Evil warps what is good. The tradition speaks of seven sins as deadly precisely because they bring destruction and death when there should be life: thus proper self-esteem, which is admirable, becomes self-absorbed pride; the natural wish to improve our circumstances becomes covetousness; joyful sexual desire is depersonalized as lust; the wise search for a richer personal life becomes envy of others who appear to have what we want; gluttony is hunger gone berserk; anger which can be the rightful protest against the ill-treatment of others, becomes another expression of damaging self-centredness; and sloth subverts the healthy need for rest into idleness. These deadly sins poison human society. When we have made allowances for mitigating circumstances, we must also accept some blame.[7]

I have no wish to create scrupulosity or stoke up feelings of guilt. Sin, serious sin, is not trivial, accidental, or coerced, which is not to suggest that less serious sin might be. But sin, first of all, involves something significant; then we have to know what we are doing; and, finally, we have to be doing it with sufficient deliberation. In traditional language, serious sin involves grave matter, full knowledge, and deliberate consent. There is a need for a degree of cool self-awareness. In other contexts, we have become familiar with the idea of someone being in denial. People whose behaviour is addictive, whether we are talking about drink or drugs, gambling or sex, whatever it may be, will never be able even to begin the process of recovery until they can acknowledge the true character of what they are doing. Addicts are brilliantly persuasive counsels for the defence, at least to their own way of thinking. It is much the same with us and sin. We find it hard to admit that we sin. But we do. Everyone does. When we can admit that to ourselves, we can begin to recognize the ways in which indeed we are not perfect, turn and ask for forgiveness, and be reconciled.

To have made that step and received sacramental absolution can often be an experience which brings extraordinary comfort and peace. Facing the truth about ourselves and in sorrow – and probably with some apprehensiveness – confessing and receiving God's pardon through the ministry of the Church is an occasion of great blessing. Many tears of relief have been shed in the celebrating of this sacrament as people have found terrible burdens which they have borne for years, lifted off them. Little by little, particularly as we celebrate the sacrament regularly, every month or two, and it becomes a part of the discipline of our spiritual lives, we find ourselves built up and renewed and so we continue to walk along the path of holiness and discipleship with surer step.

There are, naturally enough, other hazards on the way. Let me mention three of them.

The first is very common. After a while, we become demoralized because we find that every confession is virtually the same. Each time we go, we have to mention the same sins and failings and it seems as though we are making no progress. As a student long ago, I raised the subject with my own spiritual director and since then many people coming to confession have raised the question with me. I always pass on his advice.

I went in to him and said, 'I'm afraid that all I've got to tell you is the same old story.' And he replied, 'Well, I'm very pleased to hear it.' Surprise must have been written all over my face, because he laughed and went on to explain what he meant. 'Just think,' he said to me, 'what a bizarre sort of person you would be if every time you came to confession, you had a completely fresh set of sins to confess. If at first you confessed violent anger, which by the next time had vanished altogether, leaving you mild and gentle, but now, having previously been honest, you admitted to constant deliberate lying, and then after that sexual promiscuity, and so on. We are not like that. As persons we have strengths and weaknesses, and we have to struggle to overcome the weaknesses all through our lives. We want to grow, to develop, and we do; there are shifts and changes of emphasis; but you may find that you spend your whole life essentially in conflict with the same sins.' These words are full of good sense and I have often passed them on to others. They offer a wise perspective.

I have used them particularly when someone has been preparing for reception into full communion with the Church and has been about to go to confession for the first time or when someone was returning to the sacramental practice of the faith, perhaps after many years as lapsed. In those situations people are naturally anxious to celebrate their reconciliation with the utmost care, but can feel dismayed. How can they search satisfactorily the long years of their lives for all the sins they may have committed?

I reassure them. An anxious investigation of their lives with a fine-tooth comb to uncover every possible misdemeanour, however slight, is not what is asked of them. What is needed is calm, honest, prayerful self-appraisal, a search for the fundamental flaws that have separated them from God, the elements in an individual's personality which lie at the root of wrongdoing. And then, when those crucial flaws have been uncovered, we may detect the ways in which they have revealed themselves. So, for example, someone who comes to recognize that he is narrowly self-absorbed, may find there the cause for his other failings, his carelessness in prayer, bad temper with his family, excessive criticism of those at work, and even at times his cavalier negligence when driving his car.

A second hazard must also be avoided, if we are not to be snared by scruples. It is linked to that advice I received years ago, when warned about the weaknesses which we struggle to overcome throughout our lives. We have to remember that we are not asked to confess those weaknesses, but our actual sins. In other words, we do not ask pardon for our tendencies, but for the times we have turned those tendencies into action. This man may tend to moral cowardice, but in fact behave with great courage; that woman may often feel exasperated and impatient with her colleagues, but you would never know it, because she treats them always gently and with consideration; many of us may be disposed to neglect our prayers, but in spite of that be very faithful to the time we give to them. We are asked to confess only the surrender to moral cowardice, the outburst of impatience, the failure to pray, not the sinful tendencies to this behaviour which with God's help we have regularly resisted. Some will have been heroic in their resistance. We are asked to confess only our defeats.

A third hazard which may handicap us is a sense of unreality which we may sometimes feel surrounds this exercise of confession and forgiveness. At first, we are in a state of grace, as it is called, at peace with God, but we sin and so are exiled from God's favour. We confess and are forgiven, and so are returned to the state of grace. Then we sin again. Then we repent. Then we sin. The whole operation lacks credibility. We seem to be like a yo-yo, at one moment in God's hand, then falling out of it, then returned, then fallen again. And so it goes on. We need to be confident that it is not arbitrary like that, but has its own coherence. There are certain choices which shape a person's entire moral life and which create the setting within which other particular, everyday choices come to be made.[8] The whole moral enterprise is a matter of bringing those particular choices into harmony with the basic decisions which give our lives their moral shape. We have been reconciled to God in Christ. Our lives at times fail to reflect that reality. Therefore, as St Paul instructs us, we must be reconciled.[9]

This struggle for reconciliation lies at the heart of our Christian lives. We rejoice in our vocation to holiness and discipleship, but feel inadequate and unworthy. We try to bridge the gap between what we have received in Christ and our response which is too often flawed. But we are not left to our own devices. This wonderful sacrament is offered to us to help us overcome our failings and to tutor us in holiness.

(iv)

Eucharist and reconciliation sustain us. They help us to live in holiness and be faithful in discipleship. We know that we have not received this vocation to love for ourselves alone. Christian life is never primarily a private affair. Our sins not only diminish us; they also damage the Church. Reconciliation brings healing. And by the eucharist we not only come closer to Christ as individuals, but we do so by being grafted more perfectly into his body which is the Church. To realize these truths should reassure us. By celebrating these sacraments regularly, we are nurtured in holiness and given the strength to follow the call to discipleship more faithfully. We are able to bear witness to our life in Christ. We know already that our vocation to love has to be made real. People have to see this love in action.

10

Love in Action

IN his first letter to the Corinthians, St Paul composed a passage about love which has become renowned.[1] I have often heard it read out loud in church, especially at weddings. In fact, nowadays, as I listen, I also notice the mood in the congregation and am struck by the way almost invariably these words cause a stillness to rest on those who have gathered. They are extraordinary words.

Paul begins by calling attention to a number of gifts. He says that if he had such a gift for languages that he could speak every one of them, 'the tongues of men and angels', that if he had such knowledge that he could plumb the depths of the deepest truths, understanding all mysteries, that if indeed he had that kind of faith which can move mountains, and if he even were prepared to be burnt alive, but was without love, then such gifts, such faith, and such self-sacrifice would count for nothing. Without love they are worthless. And what does he mean by love? He identifies it as patient and kind, not jealous or boastful, arrogant or rude, nor selfishly stubborn or irritable or resentful, pleased when things go well and sad when they do not. Here are qualities which we commonly suppose we possess, believing ourselves to be reasonably kind and patient and not too given to sulking when we don't get our own way, and so on. We may, of course, be giving ourselves a better press than we deserve, but it is a stroke of genius on Paul's part to link that love without which exceptional gifts are worthless with ordinary, everyday aspects of human behaviour. And he concludes by reminding us that, while other talents and qualities pass away, love endures and must develop and mature in us, so that what at first is seen through a glass darkly is finally revealed in perfect and absolute radiance. Love is the bedrock of living Catholicism. And while this passage from Paul's writings is very popular at weddings, it is important for us to remember that it is not dealing with married love in particular, but Christian life in general. We are all called to love. That must be clear by now.

And in the first place, of course, we are called to love particular people. Marriage is an outstanding example of that, but all true loving is never vague or abstract. Were someone to claim to love people in general, but not specific individuals, we would be suspicious. Love must be made real in particular, personal relationships. Charity, we say, begins at home. We love our family and friends. Besides the sense in which we take that saying for granted, there is a deeper sense in which loving those closest to us and constantly about us can be extremely demanding. Most of can manage to be agreeable for an evening or a weekend. Love requires much more: faithfulness and constancy. The family is a genuine school for love. When love within the family is strong, we learn more easily the vital skills for loving. But our discipleship based on love has also to reach beyond these immediate personal relationships.

The great commandment teaches us to love God and our neighbour,[2] and these two loves are not to be divided; we remember the words from the first letter of John: 'If anyone says, "I love God," and hates his brother, he is a liar; for he who does not love his brother whom he has seen, cannot love God whom he has not seen.'[3] This is familiar teaching. But how are we to make it real? How are we to put into practice this love of our neighbour, this loving which reaches beyond our more immediate personal relationships? Perhaps we can best begin to explore its larger implications by asking again the question which a lawyer once put to Jesus: 'Who is my neighbour?'[4] It is not simply the pleasant, friendly person who lives next door.

Jesus answered by telling the parable of the good Samaritan.[5] We know it well as a story: a man travelling from Jerusalem to

Jericho was assaulted, robbed, and left for dead; a priest and a Levite passed by, but ignored him; only a Samaritan took pity on him and cared for him. All the same, we may miss the power of the reply. Samaritans were despised utterly by the Jews. One indication of that is the way the lawyer could not bring himself to identify the Samaritan as a neighbour by his name, but only by his deed, so that when Jesus came to the end of the parable and asked, 'Which of these three, do you think, proved neighbour to the man who fell among the robbers?' he would only say, 'The one who showed mercy on him.' A Jewish friend of mine once made the point by commenting that, if Jesus were telling the story in Israel today, he would not be speaking about a Samaritan, but a young Palestinian terrorist. In other words, the neighbour we are called to love is the person whom instinctively we most hate. The conclusion is unavoidable: no one is to be beyond the scope of this love. That may seem impossible and unreasonable. And so we find ourselves faced with a second question: how can we be expected to love those whom left to ourselves we hate, from whom we feel completely divided?

Here we need to remember something about loving which corresponds to a lesson we learnt about praying, namely the distinction between emotion and choice. Just as prayer is not principally a matter of how we feel, but of a decision to come close to God – we pray because we want to – this loving similarly is not primarily a question of feeling, a matter of cosy sentiment or emotion at high tide, but is something we choose to do. There may be times when we love and we find our emotions are powerfully in tune with our loving, but, more fundamental than feeling, this love is built upon a decision based on desire, on the will to love. We love, because we want to love, not simply because we feel like it. It is a disposition, shaped by choice. We choose to approach people in this way, whoever they may be and in spite of our feelings. And so we come to a third question: why should we? What is the motive that prompts the disposition to love? Why are we commanded to love? It helps to remember how the Gospels end.

Many people will know – perhaps even by heart – the ending of St Matthew's Gospel. Jesus said, 'Go therefore and make disciples of all nations, baptizing them in the name of the Father and of the Son and of the Holy Spirit, teaching them to observe all that I have commanded you.' We may, however, be less familiar with the way the other Gospels end. In the Marcan account, Jesus says, 'Go into all the world and preach the gospel to the whole creation.' St Luke describes Jesus explaining to his disciples what has happened and instructing them that 'repentance and forgiveness of sins should be preached in his name to all nations, beginning from Jerusalem.' And he adds, 'You are witnesses of these things.' And the Fourth Gospel concludes by declaring that what has been written has been written 'that you may believe that Jesus is the Christ, the Son of God, and that believing you may have life in his name'.[6] The character of these endings varies, but the essential point is common: the disciples have to spread this message because it is a message of love, charged with a power and seriousness which reaches far beyond mercurial feelings. Time and again in these pages we have recognized that the drama of human existence is a story of love: of creation by God out of love, of separation by sin from love, and of reconciliation to love through the unreserved love revealed by Jesus on the cross. Here is good news for all; love supplies its own motive; everyone should have the chance to hear it. No one should be excluded. The message is not only for those I happen to like and favour. My feelings cannot be allowed to determine who hears this news. When its influence overcomes us, we want everyone to benefit. We delight in sharing this good news. The gospel of love, revealed supremely in the death and resurrection of Jesus, must be proclaimed. That is imperative. We call it evangelization. As followers of Jesus, we have a duty to evangelize. It is an outstanding way of putting love into practice.

But first we need a word of warning and then we should recognize that evangelization is a complex, varied, and unpredictable activity.

(ii)

First, the warning. Mention of evangelization can cause alarm. It can be associated with bringing pressure to bear on people, especially perhaps on those who are weak and vulnerable. That has sadly happened at times. Some years ago a Jewish boy was put under intense pressure to convert by zealous Christian friends. He felt torn between his home, his culture, and his traditional beliefs, on the one hand, and their advocacy of the Christian gospel, on the other. He resolved his dilemma in the most tragic manner: he took his own life. And when a Christian minister was asked whether it would not have been more Christian to leave the boy alone, he was reported to have replied, 'How could it be more Christian to withhold the precious gift of the gospel?' If the report is true, the reply is scandalous. It confuses the gift with the way it is presented. It fails to distinguish between proposing the gospel and imposing it. In seeking to make the good news known, there is no place for coercion. This is false evangelization, action without love.

And, secondly, evangelization is a complex activity, which can be carried out in various ways. We usually think of it rather narrowly as instruction, whether given to an individual or a group. Priests and religious, catechists and teachers, and most of all parents will generally be the ones directly involved in this work, but all the baptized have a part to play in making the gospel known. However, the outcome will always be unpredictable, because what we seek to share is faith and faith is a gift. That is what we call it, but we do not always appreciate what it is we are saying.

Gifts make us think of presents, something we have been given. If we have it, we have it. Parents can become distressed when their children stop practising. 'How can they lose their faith?' they ask. 'They've been baptized. They've got the gift of faith.' But when we speak of faith as a gift, we are not talking about an object possessed; we are rather acknowledging the way it comes to us: as a gift, it comes to us from God freely. We do not deserve it. It is not a reward due to some merit of ours. But the fact that it is a free gift creates a further problem.

Writing to the Thessalonians, Paul once noted that 'not all have faith'.[7] And we might ask, 'Why not?' The constant theme of these reflections has been that God loves us and wishes everyone to be saved from their sins, to be reconciled to him. If the key to salvation is faith which is his free gift, then why does he not give it to all? Now Paul in fact was speaking about some trouble he was having from those who were not members of the Christian community. Not all have faith here, he was saying, and the non-believers are making it difficult for me. He was speaking rather specifically; but we can still investigate his phrase more generally: not all have faith. Some do; others don't; it all seems rather arbitrary.

There is a puzzle here. There are many fine people in the world, for whom religion means nothing. They are brimful of generosity, understanding, patience, kindness, and love, but when it comes to religion, they shake their heads. Some of them will say that they wish it were otherwise, but there is nothing they can do about it. It does not register. They cannot accept a word of it. As a university chaplain, I was often approached by those who were curious about the gospel and certainly well disposed. Many in the course of their search and inquiry came to believe, but there were always some who could not go on. They were grateful for the time spent with them and appreciative of the greater understanding they had gained, but they could go no further. They understood, but they did not believe. It is bewildering that God in his providence should withhold faith from such people, but that seems to be what happens. All the careful packaging in the world will make no difference. Faith comes as a free gift; it is not given to all. We cannot guarantee the outcome, but we try to prepare the ground. It is all a part of putting love into practice. We will consider the implications later.

Many people will applaud this work, even when success seems to be slight, in so far as it involves religious teaching in homes, classrooms, and parishes, but they become apprehensive when they find it elsewhere. Evangelization, however, can take different, less direct, forms. There are other ways of putting love into practice.

(iii)

Faith must not exist in a sealed compartment in our lives; it should permeate every situation. As we have realized already, it is not enough to love people in general; we have to love particular people in personal, immediate ways. At the same time, we must not limit our loving to individuals. We have wider responsibilities and a range of opportunities. The idea is not new. St John Chrysostom, Bishop of Constantinople and Doctor of the Church, who died in 407, once observed crisply, 'Do not honour [the body of Christ] here in church clothed in silk vestments and then pass him by unclothed and frozen outside.'[8] Pope Paul VI taught this same idea when he wrote about the contribution of the lay faithful to evangelization. He encouraged them to put to use 'every Christian and evangelical possibility latent but already present and active in the affairs of the world'. And he went on to describe their sphere of action as 'the vast and complicated world of politics, society and economics, . . . the world of culture, of the sciences and the arts, of international life, of the mass media'. He then referred to other areas which he identified as open to evangelization, 'human love, the family, the education of children and adolescents, professional work, [and] suffering'.[9] The sheer range of this activity may seem overwhelming, for the implications are very great. Here evidently our neighbour is no longer only an individual. We are thinking of a community, of society. How are we to respond? How can we put the command to love our neighbour into practice, when the sweep is so broad? One major significant resource is the wealth available to us in Catholic social teaching.

To say so, however, is precisely what can make some people apprehensive. They feel at ease with the gospel message confined to the home, the school, or the parish, but threatened when they discover it elsewhere. It makes them uncomfortable. A common reaction will be to criticize it as 'church interference in politics'. They need to take to heart Archbishop Derek Worlock's response to this charge, which echoes in our day the words of John Chrysostom. Addressing the National Conference of Priests in 1991, he said:

> My short stock answer [to the question, 'How do you justify Church interference in politics?'] is that God has commanded me to love him and my neighbour. There are some fairly obvious ways in which I can show my love for God in worship; but my love of my neighbour (and of God in my neighbour) involves my concern about his spiritual *and* his human condition. I can pray for his soul but I cannot turn my back on how he is to live: his well-being, his freedom, his prosperity or poverty, his house, his job, and so on. All that lies in the field of politics, whether I like it or not. So it is part of my double commitment, to God and neighbour, which I share with all my fellow creatures, but especially with other baptized Christians.[10]

Archbishop Worlock was speaking at a conference which marked the centenary of the encyclical letter of Pope Leo XIII, *Rerum Novarum*, on the conditions of workers. From one viewpoint that letter was a belated, overdue response to the Industrial Revolution, but from another it supplied the impulse for the formulation of Catholic social teaching which, particularly over the past forty years, successive popes have developed into an impressive and consistent approach to key social questions related to justice and peace. Its teaching is not party political, nor indeed solely Catholic in any narrow, exclusive sense. It is addressed to everyone of good will as a way to establishing a better and fairer society for the benefit of all. It seeks the common good. It has become a significant resource to enable us to put the love of our neighbour into practice.

(iv)

The origins of Catholic social teaching can be found in the second half of the nineteenth century in the clash between laissez-faire capitalism and the determinist economic laws of Marxist Socialism. That was the context in which it arose. And while its content is too rich and varied for a satisfying account of it to be given here, it may help to sketch the three main elements on which it rests: the dignity of the human person, and the principles of solidarity and subsidiarity.

The concern for the dignity of the human person is evidently significant, because it indicates at once a greater care than for the individual alone. It turns our attention to society. It arises from our belief that the human race, male and female, is made in the image and likeness of God and that, when Jesus was born, then the Word of God became flesh. Jesus was as truly divine as he was human, as truly human as he was divine. In him the relationship between the human and divine is achieved perfectly, without diminution or compromise. Therefore his humanity is not some special kind of humanity; it is ordinary humanity, just like ours; and so his birth reveals our human capacity for intimacy with God. Human dignity is fundamental. It does not depend upon some particular quality or accomplishment, race or gender, age or economic status. It is not something we achieve or which others bestow upon us. It comes from God. That conviction points to a powerful conclusion. As the Catholic Bishops of England and Wales expressed it in their statement, *The Common Good*, 'The test therefore of every institution or policy is whether it enhances or threatens human dignity and indeed human life itself. Policies which treat people as only economic units, or policies which reduce people to a passive state of dependency on welfare, do not do justice to the dignity of the human person.'[11] We have to respect the mystery and distinctiveness of every person and appreciate their value.

That sense of mystery, distinctiveness, and value gives rise to an awareness of relationship. Human beings do not live in isolation from one another. We are connected. Our common dignity unites us. The whole is greater than the sum of the individual parts. This recognition of our unity is the basis for Catholic teaching about solidarity. We see evidence of it, to borrow words from Pope John Paul II, when 'men and women in various parts of the world feel personally affected by the injustices and violations of human rights committed in distant countries, countries which perhaps they will never visit'. There is sometimes talk of 'charity fatigue', when we learn of crises around the world through television and another appeal is made. Yet people are still being wonderfully generous. Think of *Live Aid*. Think of lorry-loads of supplies going to Eastern Europe. Think of *Children in Need*. And the Pope noted that solidarity 'is not a feeling of vague compassion or shallow distress at the misfortunes of so many people, both near and far. On the contrary, it is *a firm and persevering determination* to commit oneself to the *common good*; that is to say to the good of all and of each individual, because we are *all* really responsible *for all*'.[12]

This sense of solidarity, furthermore, supplies the inspiration for the specific work for justice and peace of an organization like CAFOD. The Second Vatican Council in its Decree on the Apostolate of Lay People made a powerful declaration about the obligation to offer aid to those in need:

> Wherever men are to be found who are in want of food and drink, of clothing, housing, medicine, work, education, the means necessary for leading a truly human life, wherever there are men racked by misfortune or illness, men suffering exile or imprisonment, Christian charity should go in search of them and find them out, comfort them with devoted care and give them the helps that will relieve their needs. This obligation binds first and foremost the more affluent individuals and nations.

The basis of this action must never be self-seeking, but must rather recognize that our neighbour has been created in the image of God and of the Christ. Familiar themes return. The dignity of the person must be respected and the demands of justice satisfied. What is 'already due in justice is not to be offered as a gift of charity'. Our action must seek to eradicate the causes of evil, not merely their effects.[13]

We recognize too that we are united to others in a profound way and not only those overseas. There are those closer to home and we should not imagine that we are doing all the giving. Fr Austin Smith has lived in Liverpool 8 for almost thirty years, devoting his life to the people there. They call him 'the one who stayed'. Years ago he remarked, 'In evangelical terms, having gone to minister to the least of the brethren, the least of the brethren ministered to me.'[14] We are bound together. This is solidarity. Here too we see love in action.

When we respect the human person and value the bond of connection between persons, then we need also to consider the implications for the way action is taken. How are decisions to be made? Here the principle of subsidiarity comes into play. It has become known more generally in recent years in European politics. According to this principle, decisions are taken at the appropriate level. People sometimes fail to realize what that means. They assume it is saying that decisions which can properly be taken at a lower or more local level should be taken there and not reserved to a higher or more central authority, which is correct, but they may forget that by the same token the decisions proper to that higher authority should not be farmed out. In a school, for example, there are matters which should be dealt with by a form tutor or a head of year; the head teacher does not need to intervene. But plainly there are decisions which the head has to make and which cannot be left to more junior members of staff. It is the same in a diocese. The bishop does not have to make all the decisions about everything, while there are some decisions which have to be his alone. It will be the same in business or government, indeed wherever people are working together.

One evident consequence of this frame of reference for Catholic social teaching is to highlight the importance of democracy as an invaluable way of showing people respect and including them in the just processes of a community's life. At the same time, it is vital not to be blind to the limitations of the democratic process which must never become subject to the infallibility of the 51 per cent. Nor should the appeal to democracy be used to justify policies or a course of action which are intrinsically immoral. There is need for a system of common values. To quote from *The Common Good* again, 'If democracy is not to become a democratic tyranny in which the majority oppresses the minority, it is necessary for the public to have an understanding of the common good and the concepts that underlie it.'[15]

A natural, essential corollary to this view is respect for human rights. And it is true that we have to discern which rights are genuine. Sometimes people may try to justify their actions as rights, but not everything claimed as a right will be one in fact. There is no right, for example, to choose to harm another. Nevertheless, when that has been said, the principle must be defended 'that individuals have a claim on each other and on society for certain basic minimum conditions without which the value of human life is diminished or even negated'. These rights follow from a sense of the dignity of the human person, who has most fundamentally of all the right to life. Other rights are inextricably bound up with that one: the right to religious liberty, housing, education, health care, freedom of speech, decent work, and the right to raise and provide for a family. This range of rights illustrates the importance of avoiding pre-occupation with a single issue. Attention must be paid to them all. It becomes obvious when we recognize the absurdity of someone campaigning against capital punishment and in favour of abortion, or the other way round. The inconsistency makes no sense. These issues must not be isolated. They form a seamless robe and are linked to rights which everyone has the duty to safeguard and to ensure that the freedoms they require are respected.[16]

Moreover, we need to be aware that when these rights are

neglected, the damage that is done may not only be the work of individuals; the very structure of society may have caused the evil. Structural sin is a reality as well. In any society there will be unevenness; the position of some will be judged more advantageous than that of others; but at the same time, economic policy, domestic policy, foreign policy can be so planned that the unevenness is calculated and unjust. It lurks whenever we find ourselves asking, 'What can we little people do?' Walking to Jerusalem in 1987 as a pilgrim for peace, Fr Gerry Hughes found himself pondering that question over a beer with a barman in what was then Yugoslavia. And the nub of the response, he came to realize, was never to allow the question to become an atheistic one, as though the answer depended on ourselves. We may be able to do very little, even less than we think, but we must have faith and let God be God in our lives, so that he can make himself manifest and work through us.[17]

To mention these points – the dignity of the human person, the principles of solidarity and subsidiarity, the implications for the exercise of democracy, and the way the issues involved are interwoven for good or ill – only begins to indicate the basis of Catholic social teaching, but when our lives come gradually to be shaped by this perspective, then our neighbour is being loved, the gospel is being proclaimed, love is being put into action, and little by little a seed is being sown which can renew and transform our world. Or can it? How can it? Such a claim may seem to be so idealistic as to be preposterous. We say we are evangelizing, but what difference do we make? We speak of changing our world, but the developed world at least appears to have little interest in the kind of change which we have in mind: it is not returning to faith in the gospel or seeking that renewal which could transform it. It may help if we check our expectations.

(v)

When we try to make love real in action, we seek to spread the gospel so that people may grow in holiness. This is what is meant by evangelization and sanctification. But what do we imagine the effects of our evangelizing and sanctifying would be, were we successful? Would it mean worldwide conversion to committed Christianity? Forget about the world for a moment. Think about the place where you live, the village, town, city or suburb. Then imagine that place wholly converted to Christianity: every resident and everyone who came to work there, every politician, every doctor, every lawyer, every teacher, every policeman, every shop-owner and everyone who worked in those shops, every tradesman, every gardener, every bricklayer, every joiner, plumber, and electrician, every single man, woman, and child, not only professing the Christian faith, but deeply and sincerely committed to it and attempting to live it as fully and as graciously as possible. Imagine it. I suspect the imagination reels. So is our duty to evangelize doomed to failure? No, it is not.

Remember the images of salt and light, and of the leaven.[18] These, I suggest, are the clues to follow. They help us see what our evangelizing should be like. Like leaven, like salt and light, we are not the whole, but a vital part of the whole. As there is more to a loaf than its leaven, more to a meal than the pinch of salt which flavours it, and more to a room's decoration than its light bulb, so there will be more to human society than the Christian community. But as a loaf without leaven will not rise, and a meal without salt will be tasteless, and a room without light useless, so a world without the gospel will be lifeless. And here the implications of faith as gift may become clearer to us. For those of us who have received this gift need to be aware that we have a responsibility when we remember that it is a gift, and not a reward.

We who believe without merit must take after the Son of man who came not to be served, but to serve, and to give his life as a ransom for many.[19] We must let the gift of faith so possess us that what we have received is not only a blessing on us, but a service to others, a gift held in trust for them. Part of our putting love into practice is believing on their behalf. We believe for them.

This notion may seem odd and, indeed, arrogant, but when we understand it correctly, we will recognize that it is not. We come to realize that we receive as well as give. When I think about this issue, I always remember Claire Lawrence.

I buried Claire in the early spring of 1990. She was very young, just over four years old. She had been born with cerebral palsy which made her a prey to meningitis, epilepsy, pneumonia, and any other passing virus; she never spoke, was probably deaf, and almost certainly blind; but, although she was virtually incapable of any response at all, she received unending love from the doctors and nurses who cared for her, the teachers who worked with her, the family friends who came to visit her, and most of all from her mother and father. Now I do not wish to be misunderstood. I am not suggesting that Claire's terrible disabilities supply an analogy for the non-Christian world, which can simply be dismissed as deaf, dumb, and blind, and burdened with disease. That idea would be arrogant, and as false as it is arrogant. Whatever claims we might wish to make for the Christian gospel, we cannot presume to determine how else God may make himself known. I wish simply to use one aspect of her condition, the fact that she could not actually respond. And in our world there is the fact that many, though full of goodwill, cannot respond to the gospel with faith. Yet, as Claire was surrounded by love and received love, so all men and women can be touched by faith, if those who believe will do so on their behalf.

And this relationship is not all one-way. When Claire died, many people acknowledged that she had tapped depths in their capacity for love of which, before knowing her, they had been unaware. In this way, she not only received love from them, but returned it as well. Could it not be the same for those of us who believe, when we truly care about those who do not? We can believe on their behalf and with no trace of condescension. On the contrary, we find ourselves enriched, because we discover that our own faith has been deepened, inspired, so to speak, by their incapacity. We believe for them. When we show love in action, we may not find that our example leads to mass conversion, but the faith, maturing in us, may come to be of service to all.

(vi)

Earlier we reflected on prayer as simple; now we recognize that putting love into practice is complex. We may call it evangelization, but its character varies in relation to family and friends, and in relation to neighbours as individuals, but also as community, as part of a larger society. We are called to live our Catholicism in an untidy world, as a leaven. We try to give a service which makes a difference and brings a blessing, renewal, and transformation. Living Catholicism requires living witness. According to an old saying, we are to be 'in the world, but not of the world'. But what does that mean? It is a saying which repays careful scrutiny.

11

Living Witness

(i)

WE are all familiar with the trite observation that cemeteries are full of indispensable people. Some of them never the less are greatly missed. We know that their early, untimely death has deprived us of gifts we need. Such a person was Bishop Francis Thomas of Northampton, who died on Christmas Day in 1988. I met him only once. He was the Bishops' Conference liaison bishop for university chaplains and came to Oxford in 1987, when the chaplaincy there hosted the Chaplains' Conference. He said little, but his grasp of the essential points of our discussion was formidable.

Before the cancer which killed him became known, he had accepted an invitation to deliver the Third Cottesloe Annual Lecture in Buckingham. He was to speak on 7 October 1988, but it became clear that he would be too sick to do so. I was honoured to be asked to take his place. The organisers were kindness itself. They did everything they could to accommodate me at short notice, even offering to change the title of the lecture, if it would help me. But since posters had gone out and advertisements been printed, I preferred to keep to the title which Bishop Thomas had agreed: 'In the world, but not of the world'. I have never regretted the decision. It raises neatly the question of the setting within which we are called to bear living witness to the gospel; it can help us identify the pressures that witness involves for us and our capacity to bear them; and it can lead us again to recognize that we must place ourselves in God's hands.

(ii)

As part of my preparation, I inquired of various people where they thought this well-known saying, the title of my sudden lecture, had come from. I received a range of replies. Some backed St Paul, others St John, and there were those who narrowed their eyes, suspicious of the trick question, and decided on St Augustine. But the truth is more surprising: no one knows the origin of the phrase. The nearest we can find is an observation in the Epistle to Diognetus, written about the year 124, which declared, 'Christians inhabit the world, but they are not part of the world.'[1] However, the inspiration is probably Johannine. In his discourse at the Last Supper in the Fourth Gospel, Jesus concludes with a passage we have come to call his High Priestly Prayer. Speaking to his Father in heaven, he says, 'And now I am no more in the world, but they [the disciples] are in the world, . . . and the world has hated them because they are not of the world, even as I am not of the world.'[2] This Johannine link is instructive. When this Gospel speaks of the world, we detect an ambiguity.

In this prayer the world is identified with what is hostile to Jesus and his mission. And so those who follow Jesus are also hated by the world. They live in enemy territory, in the midst of that hostility. They are not of the world, even as Jesus is not of the world. From this opposition a spirituality has developed which despises the world. It regards the world with contempt. When we look more closely, however, we realize that that attitude tells us only one side of the story.

The world which is hostile, is also beloved. Earlier in the Gospel we have been taught that 'God so loved the world that he gave his only Son, that whoever believes in him should not perish but have eternal life.' The Son came 'not to condemn the world, but that the world might be saved through him.'[3] There are not two worlds, one which is hostile and the other beloved. It is the same world. This ambiguity characterizes the setting within which we have to live our Catholicism.

We must be witnesses, but it is not easy to make out the lie of the land. More recently the scene has changed. Tony Philpot, priest, preacher, and writer, has called it 'uncharted territory'. He has reflected on the conditions within which ordained priests have to exercise their ministry these days, but his remarks can be applied more broadly to include all those who are trying to live their faith. He describes the hostile world, as it is today; in a memorable phrase, he calls it one 'whose belief-muscles have atrophied'.[4] Earlier Catholic heroes confronted fierce opposition clearly defined by alternative beliefs or convictions. Remember the martyrs of England and Wales, Scotland and Ireland. Our circumstances are different. It is less a matter of conflict and more, as he says, a kind of 'exile'. And he captures neatly the ambiguity of our situation. He writes:

> It isn't that we are unhappy in a world of TV and con-
> venience food and dishwashers and the internet. We haven't
> recoiled from the technological culture, or the comfort and
> convenience it gives us, quite the reverse. But we know,
> and preach, that the electronic revolution and the constantly
> improving chip cannot fulfil the needs of the human soul.
> To this extent we are oddities, and exiles on our own soil.
> Yet this is where we have to sing the song of the Lord:
> there is no other place.[5]

There is no other place. And our lives, our discipleship, and our witness, if they are to bear fruit, must also be at home in this world.

To say that is not to encourage giving in, as Tony Philpot puts it, to the 'temptation to surrender, to become like other people, to adopt the language and the values and thought-patterns of the people around us'.[6] It is a question once more of the incarnation. Jesus was not a divine visitor, disguised in humanity. He was as truly human as he was divine. This world was his world. It follows that our share in his life must not be at the expense of our humanity. Our spirituality and our living witness must engage with our world, our surroundings, our conditions. In that sense, it is not enough to be in the world, but not of it; we have to be both in the world *and of the world*. As aliens, we can never reclaim it. We have to be at home here if we are to bear witness effectively.

Such is the setting, marked by ambiguity, for the witness we must bear. It can help us identify the pressures which are involved. This discipleship, as we should now expect, is costly. The struggle to remain faithful in these circumstances will often drain us.

(iii)

To live in a society whose belief-muscles have atrophied may be new, but the struggle with ambiguity is as old as the gospel. The conflict between what is hostile to God and what is beloved takes place, first of all, within our own hearts and minds and wills. Think of St Paul, writing to the Romans, and expounding the tension between the law and the Spirit. There are depths and technicalities to this discussion, but there is also an appeal to his personal experience which anyone can recognize: 'I do not do the good I want, but the evil I do not want is what I do.'[7] I suspect we can all recognize that: we know what is good and wish to act accordingly, but that wish alone will not guarantee the outcome. We may still do the very opposite. I am not thinking of sin so much as the ordering of our daily lives: when we get up and go to bed; how much we eat and drink; the time we give to work and relaxation, and how we spend it. The struggle to live in harmony with the gospel begins within us in very ordinary ways.

For me the outstanding account of this struggle has been given by Pope Gregory the Great, who was summoned from monastic life to the papacy in a time of plague. It was Gregory who sent Augustine to England and supported him on that mission. In one of his homilies he speaks of his own situation. He is self-critical. To some extent he echoes Paul: 'I do not preach as I should nor does my life follow the principles I preach

so inadequately.' He mentions the many responsibilities which
have been laid on him and how their sheer number frustrates
his concentration, and then continues:

> I am often compelled by the nature of my position to
> associate with men of the world and sometimes I relax the
> discipline of my speech. If I preserved the rigorously inflex-
> ible mode of utterance that my conscience dictates, I know
> that the weaker sort of men would recoil from me and that
> I could never attract them to the goal I desire for them.
> So I must frequently listen patiently to their aimless chatter.
> Because I am weak myself I am gradually drawn into idle
> talk and I find myself saying the kind of thing that I didn't
> even care to listen to before. I enjoy lying back where I
> once was loath to stumble.[8]

Gregory died in 604. Our attitudes and standards may be different
in many ways, but we can sympathize with his dilemma. His
concern to bring people to God – to attract them to the goal
he desires for them – involves him in a kind of compromise – he
relaxes the discipline of his speech – which in time he comes to
enjoy. To be a living witness is an untidy, messy business.

Whenever I think of Gregory's dilemma, I am reminded of a
passage from one of Newman's Anglican sermons which seems
to be its natural companion. It is a startling piece. He is con-
sidering the way God's purpose for the Church is worked out
through human infirmity and sin. 'What is true of the Church
as a body,' he then remarks, 'is true also of each member of it
who fulfils his calling.' He is speaking of someone who is holy:
'Could we see his soul as Angels see it, he would, when seen at
a distance, appear youthful in countenance, and bright in apparel;
but approach him, and his face has lines of care upon it, and his
dress is tattered.' On closer inspection the young face is found
to be strained and the elegant clothes are torn. However, this
man's condition, Newman says, is not superficial, 'but, as it were,
wrought out of sin, the result of a continual struggle, – not
spontaneous nature, but habitual self-command.' And he goes

on, 'True faith is not shown here below in peace, but rather in conflict; . . . we arrive at holiness through infirmity, because man's very condition is a fallen one, and in passing out of the country of sin, he necessarily passes through it.'[9] There is a puritanical element in this sermon which needs to be qualified, but it remains nevertheless an eloquent expression of the struggle in which we are engaged, when we seek to bear witness to our faith. Not everything goes according to plan. Even Jesus discovered that.

I take comfort from a moment in the Gospel when the twelve have just returned from their first experience of mission. Jesus had sent them out two by two. When they return and report back to him, filled no doubt with enthusiasm, he suggests that they go off to a lonely place to rest for a while. But the people see them leaving, guess where they are going, and get there ahead of them. We are told that, when Jesus arrived, he had compassion on the crowds and began to teach them. The incident has been used to illustrate his tirelessness. I take comfort because it also illustrates that the Lord's plans could be thwarted as well. After all, the idea had been to go away for a quiet time and to reflect. It was wonderful to care for the crowds, but his intention had been to care for the disciples.[10]

We cannot foretell what demands will be made of us or their consequences. On one occasion, when I tried to explain the dilemmas and apparent complexities of daily Christian life in a homily using this incident, I was rebuked later by a parishioner as a bad priest who was preaching complacency. But to be aware of complexity and to make allowances is not softness. When we try to show sensitivity to particular pastoral needs, not laying on people burdens which can only crush them, we are not encouraging complacency, but following the example the Lord gave us. As St Gregory realized, it is possible to proclaim the truth in a fine way, but cause harm, because the people we wish to win over, will not understand. Inappropriate language and behaviour, however accurate and correct from one perspective, may erect barriers which gentler words and actions would never have raised.

It is easy to see how demanding this life can be. As we seek to live Catholicism in an ambiguous setting, we may well become worn down. We wonder whether we have given in to compromise. At times we may seem to do nothing but fail. We feel discouraged, depressed, and inadequate. It is important not to lose heart. We must be sure to place ourselves in the Lord's hands. We find ourselves once more in the company of Bartimaeus. But he has a further lesson to illustrate for us.

(iv)

On retreat in 1993, I was puzzling over the demands of discipleship. One day I was given a text from the Fourth Gospel to prompt my prayer. It comes from the discourse at the Last Supper. Jesus was speaking to the twelve and telling them, 'If you abide in me, and my words abide in you, ask whatever you will, and it will be done for you.'[11] I had to hear these words as addressed to me. The promise is wonderful, but I asked myself what it meant really. What does it mean to abide in Jesus and have his words abiding, at home, in me? And, linked with this text, I had been asked also to notice some words in the prophecy of Jeremiah: 'You will seek me and find me; when you seek me with all your heart, I will be found by you, says the Lord'.[12] Taken together, Jeremiah seems to suggest that abiding in Jesus involves seeking him with all my heart. In notes I made at the time I asked, 'What will that mean? What will it demand?' I was elated by the promise, but also quite frightened. What effort is implied by seeking him with all my heart? What would I have to do? What were the implications and what would be the consequences? I prayed about it, wrestled with it, left it, and came back to it.

Late the following morning, after several hours pondering these texts, I noticed something about the words of Jeremiah which had not occurred to me before. There is a shift from the

active to the passive voice. He does not say, 'When you seek me
with all your heart, you will find me', as someone might say,
'When you work hard, you will achieve success'; then success
depends on hard work, is put in proportion to it. Instead he
says, 'When you seek me with all your heart, I will *be found* by
you.' A condition is being laid down for finding the Lord: we
must seek him with all our hearts; but it is, so to speak, a
condition without proportionality. Finding the Lord does not
depend on my effort. There is a condition and that is the
wholehearted seeking; but nothing I can do, however wholehearted, can bring me to deserve to find the Lord. I must seek
with my whole heart and then I will be found by him; he will
show himself and the finding is sheer gift.

Doesn't Bartimaeus illustrate this lesson for us? We can think
of him in his blindness, sitting by the walls of Jericho and
wondering about this Jesus of whom he had heard. How he
must have longed to meet him. He sought him indeed with all
his heart; there was no other way; his blindness made it impossible for him to do anything else; he could not go and look for
Jesus. But Jesus came to him. Bartimaeus was found by Jesus. If
we seek him wholeheartedly, we will be found by him. We are
not alone. He is with us.

(v)

To be found is not at once to be perfected. As disciples and
witnesses, we have to desire to come close to God. That is
crucial. Time and again, we have discovered the importance of
desire. It is the heart of prayer, of holiness, of discipleship, and
of service in the Church of the world. The desire is the fruit of
a deep decision, independent of feeling. To say that, we have
learnt, is not to despise feeling. When feeling corresponds to
decision, it is wonderful. What can be better than to discover
that what we have to do and what we feel like doing are perfectly
in step. But feeling must not control action. We act according
to our decision, not our mood. Our lives are changed. We

seek to become as possessed by love as Jesus was. That will make our witness come alive. We must be faithful. That will form us as the kind of people whom Pope Paul VI described as those who speak to the world of a God whom they know and with whom they are familiar, as if they could see the invisible.[13]

Once again, the prospect may daunt us. How can we bear that kind of witness? We know we are unworthy and we *feel* inadequate, but we must not falter. We can be encouraged by Jock Dalrymple's reassuring words:

> Christian action, then, is done by you and me, ordinary people with weak and wobbly hearts who do not have the security of trained skills, . . . I think Christian action and the promotion of the kingdom is done by those who are afraid of what people will say, who are a bit cowardly, who are a bit diffident about standing up in public, do not have the security of plenty of practice and experience, can be capsized by failure, hurt by remarks, hurt by being ignored; find themselves reacting jealously when they do not want to, are overcome with despair, yet go on loving and trusting. It is the weak and wobbly hearts that Christ chooses, as he chose Peter, James, John, Thomas – all the disciples. They were not the high-fliers of Galilee or Judaea, they were the ordinary folk, capable of love.[14]

There is a profile of those who bear witness to the gospel which many of us can recognize. We recognize ourselves. We seem to ourselves so unsuitable for the task, bogged down, and floundering. But we press on in spite of our weaknesses. The Lord can fashion our inadequacies to his purpose. We are ordinary people, but by God's grace there is growing in us a capacity for love which leads to life.

Notes

Preface

1. Roderick Strange, *The Catholic Faith* (Oxford, 1986; London, 2001).

1. Watching for God

1. Michael Paul Gallagher, *Where is your God?* (London, 1991), pp. 17–18. The story was written by a student friend of Gallagher's.
2. J.H. Newman, *Sermons on Subjects of the Day*, uniform edition (Westminster, Maryland, 1968), pp. 278–9.
3. C.S. Dessain and Thomas Gornall SJ (eds.), *The Letters and Diaries of John Henry Newman* xxx (Oxford, 1976), p. 446. Wilfrid Ward, *The Life of John Henry Cardinal Newman* ii (London, 1912), p. 247.
4. See below, pp. 13–14.
5. See 1 Corinthians 2:12.
6. Mark 10:13–15; see Matthew 19:13–15; Luke 18:15–17.
7. Matthew 18:3.
8. Alec Guinness, *Blessings in Disguise* (London, 1985), p. 36.
9. See Mark 10:46–52.
10. See Archbishop Anthony Bloom, *Living Prayer* (London, 1966), pp. 46–8.
11. ibid., p. 47.
12. Psalm 90:12.

2. Prayer

1. If you want to catch a clear impression of Pat Rorke, see John Harriott's tribute, 'A Priest to Remember', in *The Tablet*, 15 September 1990.
2. Wendy Mary Beckett, 'Simple Prayer', *The Clergy Review* lxiii (February, 1978), pp. 42–5; quotation at p. 43.
3. ibid., p. 43.
4. See John Dalrymple, *Simple Prayer* (London, 1984), pp. 26–7; quotation at p. 26.
5. See 1 Samuel 3:1–14.
6. Dalrymple, *Simple Prayer*, pp. 97–8.

7. See, for example, John Chapman, *Spiritual Letters* (London, 1959), p. 109; also p. 25.
8. Ignatius, *Epistle to the Romans* 7, in Maxwell Staniforth (ed.), *Early Christian Writings* (Penguin Classics, 1968), p. 106.
9. Letter from S.B., 6 June 1999.
10. Chapman, *Spiritual Letters*, p. 58.
11. Herbert McCabe, *God Matters* (London, 1987), p. 223.
12. *Catechism of the Catholic Church*, n. 2560.
13. 1 Thessalonians 5:14, 17.
14. Luke 11:9.
15. James 4:3.
16. James 4:8.
17. Jane Taupin died on 13 August 1999.

3. Jesus at Prayer

1. See Mark 1:21–34; Luke 4:31–41.
2. Mark 1:35.
3. Luke 6:12.
4. Mark 6:46; Matthew 14:23.
5. Mark 1:12–13.
6. See Matthew 1:23; 2:6, 15, 18, 23.
7. Matthew 3:3; see Isaiah 40:3.
8. Deuteronomy 9:9; see Exodus 34:28.
9. Deuteronomy 6:4–5.
10. Matthew 4:3.
11. Deuteronomy 8:3; see Matthew 4:4.
12. Matthew 4:5–6.
13. See Numbers 20:2–13; Exodus 17:2–7.
14. Matthew 4:7; Deuteronomy 6:16.
15. Matthew 4:10; Deuteronomy 6:13.
16. See Luke 9:51.
17. Matthew 4:1.
18. Luke 4:1.
19. See Luke 4:3–12.
20. Luke 4:13.
21. 1 Kings 19:8.
22. See Matthew 17:1–9; Mark 9:2–10; Luke 9:28–36.
23. Luke 9:35.
24. Matthew 17:10–12; see Mark 9:11–13.
25. Mark 14:32–6.
26. See Luke 23:35, 37, 39.
27. Luke 22:26.

28. Luke 22:3.
29. Luke 22:53.
30. Herbert McCabe, *God Matters* (London, 1987), p. 219.

4. Jesus and Love

1. Mark 1:15.
2. See Mark 8:27–30; see also Mark 1:34; 9:9.
3. Mark 12:28–31; see Deuteronomy 6:4–5; Leviticus 19:18.
4. Geza Vermes, *Jesus the Jew* (London, 1983), p. 224.
5. See p. 27.
6. See Mark 1:21–34.
7. See Mark 6:30–4.
8. See Mark 8:31; Matthew 16:21; 17:22–3; 20:17–19; Luke 17:25; Matthew 17:12; 26:2.
9. See 1 Kings 3:16–27.
10. John 15:13.
11. See Mark 15:34; Matthew 27:46.
12. See John Dalrymple, *Costing Not Less Than Everything* (London, 1975), pp. 120–3.
13. See Herbert McCabe, *God Matters* (London, 1987), p. 48: 'The divine omniscience of Jesus, for example, does not conflict with his human ignorance, for divine knowledge is not in the same universe of discourse as human knowledge. For Jesus to be omniscient is nothing other than for him to be divine; it is not a question of being better informed than a non-omniscient being.'

    See also p. 59: 'Whatever we can mean by speaking of God's knowledge, we know that it cannot mean that God is well informed, that he assents to a large number of true statements. Jesus's knowledge of history, as Son of God, was no different from the existence of the world; it was not in the same ball-game with what he learnt as man.'
14. 1 Corinthians 13:4–6.
15. See Mark 8:34.
16. Elie Wiesel, *Night* (New York, 1986), pp. 61–2.
17. See Elisabeth Luard, *Family Life* (Corgi Books, 1996), p. 274. See also Nicholas Luard, *The Field of the Star* (London, 1998).
18. Basil Hume, *The Mystery of the Cross* (London, 1998), p. 20.

5. Risen in Glory to New Life

1. See Mark 5:21–43; Matthew 9:18–26; Luke 8:40–56; Luke 7:11–17; John 11:1–44.
2. See Luke 24:13–35.
3. See John 20:11–18.

4. See John 20:19–20.
5. John 21:7.
6. *Catechism of the Catholic Church*, n. 645.
7. James Alison, *Knowing Jesus* (London, 1993), p. 15.
8. ibid., p. 19.
9. ibid., p. 21.
10. See Romans 6:3–4.
11. See Matthew 28:1–10; Mark 16:1–7; Luke 24:1–12.
12. See Luke 24:10–12.
13. See John 20:3–9. See *Catechism of the Catholic Church*, n. 640.
14. See Mark 16:14.
15. See John 20:24–9.
16. See John 11:1–16.
17. See John 21:1–14.
18. John 21:15, 16, 17.
19. Mark 10:45.
20. John 15:5, 8.
21. See John Dalrymple, *Letting Go in Love* (London, 1986), pp. 129–30.
22. John 15:4.
23. Dr Elizabeth Kubler-Ross in a broadcast talk published in *The Listener*, 29 September 1983, vol. 110, no. 2828; quoted in John V. Taylor, *A Matter of Life and Death* (London, 1986), p. 35.

6. The Church as Communion

1. See Acts 2:1–4.
2. Henri de Lubac, *Catholicism* (London, 1949), p. 17 (my italics).
3. Romans 12:15.
4. See Peter Hebblethwaite, *John XXIII, Pope of the Council* (London, 1984), pp. 459–60.
5. See *Lumen Gentium*, n. 6.
6. See *Lumen Gentium*, nn.15–16.
7. Raymond E. Brown, *The Churches the Apostles Left Behind* (London, 1984), pp. 60, 74.
8. *Synod Report*, Catholic Truth Society (London, 1986), p. 15.
9. *Lumen Gentium*, n. 9.
10. *Unitatis Redintegratio*, n. 3.
11. Pope Paul VI, quoted in *Christifideles Laici*, n.19; see Norman Tanner SJ (ed.), *Decrees of the Ecumenical Councils* ii (London, Washington, 1990) p. 910.
12. *Christifideles Laici*, n. 18.
13. See Pat Jones, 'Collaborative Ministry', *Briefing*, 24 September 1992, vol. 22, pp. 4–9; quotation at p. 5. The entire address is outstanding,

rich and succinct. I acknowledge gladly the influence it has had on what I am writing here.

14. *The Sign We Give*, Report from the Working Party on Collaborative Ministry, 1995, p. 21.

15. See Vicky Cosstick, 'The Experience of Collaboration', *Briefing*, 8 October 1992, vol. 22, pp. 6–13. This address is the ideal complement to the one given by Pat Jones. Again, I gladly acknowledge my indebtedness.

16. See above, pp. 23–4.

17. See Cosstick, 'The Experience of Collaboration', p. 8.

18. See above, p. 20.

19. See above, p. 14. The quotation is the opening words of Gerard Manley Hopkins' poem, 'The Wreck of the Deutschland'.

20. It was difficult for Paul as well. He had prepared the ceremonies and then had to step back and allow me to preside at their actual celebration. Here is a clear illustration of that maturity which takes responsibility, but also allows others to take theirs.

21. John 15:5.

7. Providence and Miracles

1. J. H. Newman, *Meditations and Devotions* (London, 1893), p. 400.

2. See above, p. 47.

3. Matthew 12:39.

4. See *Catechism of the Catholic Church*, n. 548.

5. See Mark 6:5–6; Matthew 13:58.

6. I use this incident concerning Padre Pio, not to imply that everything told about him can be explained in such a way, but because his life is a source of so many genuinely remarkable stories. It seemed helpful to use an exception.

8. Holiness and Discipleship

1. Leviticus 19:1–2.

2. See Matthew 5:43–8.

3. Juan Mascaró (ed.), *Lamps of Fire* (London, 1972), p. 75.

4. See Mark 10:17–31, 35–45, 46–52; Matthew 19:16–30; 20:20–8, 29–34; Luke 18:18–30; 18:35–43 – there is no account of the second conversation in Luke.

5. Matthew 19:21.

6. See Mark 5:1–19.

7. Matthew 19:23–4.

8. St Francis de Sales, *Introduction to the Devout Life* (London, 1962), p. 11.

9. See Mark 10:30.
10. See Mark 10:35–40.
11. See above, p. ix.
12. See C.S. Dessain (ed.), *The Letters and Diaries of John Henry Newman*, vol. xx (Oxford, 1976), pp. 501–2.
13. J. H. Newman, *Autobiographical Writings* (London, 1956), pp. 254–5.
14. Mark 10:50–1.
15. Mark 10:45.
16. See pp. 107–22.
17. Leviticus 19:1–2.
18. See Leviticus 19:1–18; Mark 12:31.
19. See Matthew 25:31–46.
20. 1 Corinthians 12:27.

9. Eucharist and Reconciliation

1. See above, pp. 42–4.
2. See Ecclesiastes 3:1–8. See Albert Nolan, *Jesus before Christianity* (London, 1977), pp. 73–5.
3. Herbert McCabe, *The New Creation* (London, 1964), p. 73.
4. See Herbert McCabe, *God Matters* (London, 1987), p. 219.
5. Sheila Cassidy, 'Seventy times seven', *The Tablet*, 2 March 1991, p. 267.
6. Luke 7:36–50.
7. See Kenneth Slack, *The Seven Deadly Sins* (London, 1985). This small book offers a sharply penetrating analysis of its subject. I have relied on it heavily in this paragraph.
8. See Pope John Paul II, *Veritatis Splendor*, n. 65.
9. See 2 Corinthians 5:18–20.

10. Love in Action

1. See 1 Corinthians 13:1–13.
2. See Matthew 22:34–40; Mark 12:28–34; Luke 10:25–8.
3. 1 John 4:20.
4. Luke 10:29.
5. See Luke 10:29–37.
6. Matthew 28:19–20; Mark 16:15; Luke 24:47–8; John 20:31.
7. 2 Thessalonians 3:2.
8. St John Chrysostom, *Homily* 50,3; see Week 21 of the Year, Saturday, *The Divine Office* iii (London, 1974), pp. 480–1.
9. *Evangelii Nuntiandi*, n. 70.
10. Derek Worlock, 'Priests and Politics: Evangelisation and the Social Gospel', in *Briefing*, 26 September 1991, vol. 21, p. 6.

11. See *The Common Good and the Catholic Church's Social Teaching*, A Statement by the Catholic Bishops' Conference of England and Wales, 1996, n. 13. This Statement is a valuable distillation of Catholic social teaching and I have used it extensively to give shape to this section.
12. Pope John Paul II, *Sollicitudo Rei Socialis*, n. 38.
13. *Apostolicam Actuositatem*, n. 8.
14. Austin Smith, *Passion for the Inner City* (London, 1983), p. 73.
15. See *The Common Good*, nn. 34–5.
16. See *The Common Good*, nn. 36–7.
17. See Gerard W. Hughes, *Walk to Jerusalem: in Search of Peace* (London, 1991), pp. 172–4.
18. See Matthew 5:13,14; 13:33; *Apostolicam Actuositatem*, n. 2.
19. See Mark 10:45.

11. Living Witness

1. See Epistle to Diognetus 6.3, in *Early Christian Writings* (Penguin Classics, 1968), p. 177.
2. John 17:11, 14.
3. See John 3:16–17.
4. Tony Philpot, *Priesthood in Reality* (Bury St Edmunds, 1998), p. 55.
5. ibid., p. 53.
6. ibid., p. 53.
7. Romans 7:19.
8. Pope St Gregory the Great, *Homilies on the book of Ezekiel*, Book I, II, 4–6; quoted in *The Divine Office* iii (London, 1974), pp. 232*-3*.
9. J. H. Newman, *Parochial and Plain Sermons* v, uniform edition (Westminster, Maryland, 1967), p. 210.
10. See Mark 6:30–4; above, p. 40.
11. John 15:7.
12. Jeremiah 29:13–14.
13. See *Evangelii Nuntiandi*, n. 76.
14. John Dalrymple, *Letting Go in Love* (London, 1986), p. 132.

Index

Main discussions are indicated in italics